Concepts in Ethology

CONCEPTS IN ETHOLOGY
Animal Behavior and Bioethics

MICHAEL W. FOX, D.Sc., Ph.D., B.Vet.Med., M.R.C.V.S.

Foreword by
RENÉ DUBOS, Ph.D.

second edition

KRIEGER PUBLISHING COMPANY
MALABAR, FLORIDA
1998

Original Edition 1974
Second Edition 1998

Printed and Published by
**KRIEGER PUBLISHING COMPANY
KRIEGER DRIVE
MALABAR, FLORIDA 32950**

Copyright © 1974 by the University of Minnesota
Rights transferred to author 1996
Copyright (c) 1998 (new material) by Krieger Publishing Company

All rights reserved. No part of this book may be reproduced in any form or by any means, electronic or mechanical, including information storage and retrieval systems without permission in writing from the publisher.
No liability is assumed with respect to the use of the information contained herein.
Printed in the United States of America.

FROM A DECLARATION OF PRINCIPLES JOINTLY ADOPTED BY A COMMITTEE OF THE AMERICAN BAR ASSOCIATION AND A COMMITTEE OF PUBLISHERS:
This publication is designed to provide accurate and authoritative information in regard to the subject matter covered. It is sold with the understanding that the publisher is not engaged in rendering legal, accounting, or other professional service. If legal advice or other expert assistance is required, the services of a competent professional person should be sought.

Library of Congress Cataloging-in-Publication Data

Fox, Michael W., 1937-
    Concepts in ethology: animal behavior and bioethics / Michael W. Fox; foreword by René Dubos.—2nd ed.
        p. cm.
    Includes bibliographical references (p.   ) and index.
    ISBN 1-57524-044-0 (hardcover: alk. paper)
    1. Animal behavior. 2. Bioethics. 3. Animal welfare. I. Title.
QL751.F794 1998
591.5-dc21   97-10736
                                                                              CIP

10   9   8   7   6   5   4   3   2

The first edition of this book was the second monograph in the series of the Wesley W. Spink Lectures on Comparative Medicine, established in honor of Dr. Spink's wide range of accomplishments in comparative medicine at the University of Minnesota, where he was Regents' Professor Emeritus of Medicine and Comparative Medicine.

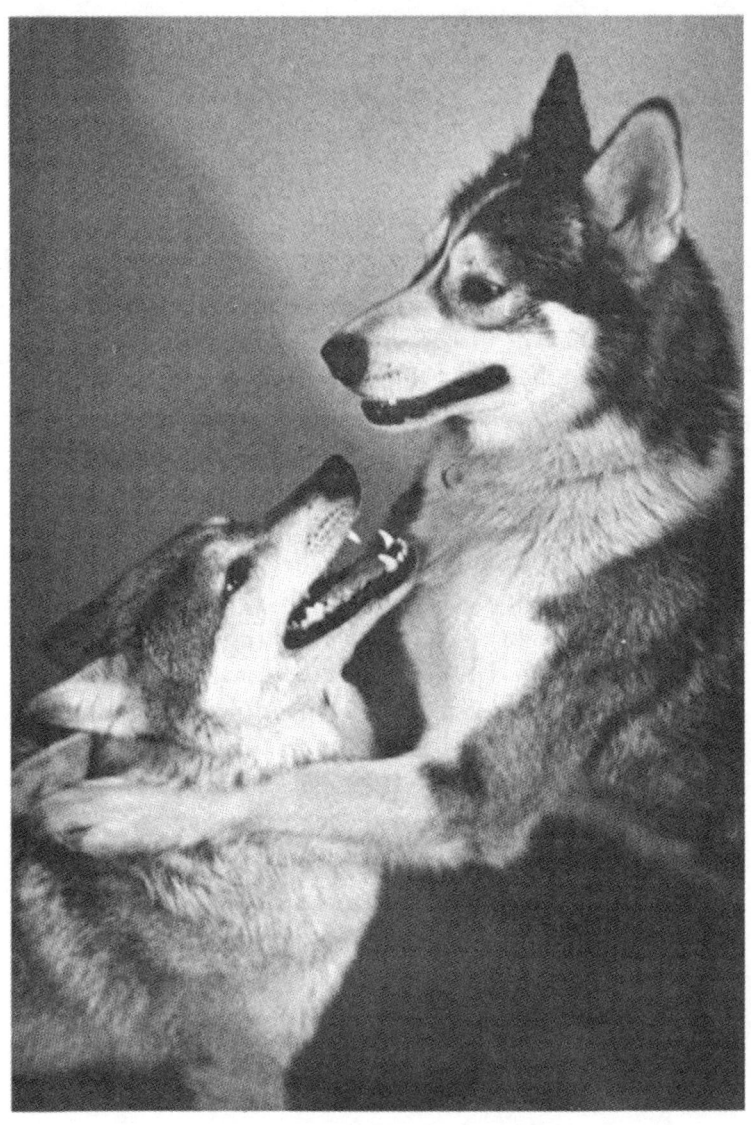

A malemute hugs a wolf during courtship. The facial expressions are examples of the open-mouth play face.

CONTENTS

FOREWORD ix

INTRODUCTION TO SECOND EDITION xix

1 ETHOLOGY—THE STUDY OF MAN AND BEAST 3

   The Beginnings of Ethology, 3

   Applied Ethology, 5

      Displacement Behaviors and Compromise Postures, 12; Derived Activities, 16; Body Language and Metacommunication, 19; Chemical Communication, 22; Space and Territory, 24

   Conclusions, 26

2 THE BEHAVIOR OF WOLVES, DOGS, AND MAN 30

   Temperament and Status in Canids, 33

   Social Behavior and Communication, 38

   Animal and Human Hunting Groups, 46

   Domestication and Civilization, 49

3 NORMAL AND ABNORMAL BEHAVIOR DEVELOPMENT 55

   Imprinting and Socialization, 56

   Early Experiences and Development, 62

Environmental Enrichment and Deprivation, 71

Social Isolation and Development, 73

Genetic and Family Influences, 78

4 APPLIED ETHOLOGY 83

Ethology and Animal Science, 83

Ethology and Laboratory Animals, 92

Behavioral Considerations in Routine Experimental Procedures, 97; Other Factors Affecting Experimental Variables, 108; Effects of Environmental Change, 110

5 ANIMAL FEELINGS AND FEELING FOR ANIMALS: HEALING THE BOND 113

Healing Animals, Animal Healing, 116

Humaneness Pays, 120

Postscript: Animal Rights and Human Liberation, 124

Animals on the Global Agenda of Human Concern and Responsibility, 130

Notes, 130

6 THE BIOETHICS OF ANIMAL AND ENVIRONMENTAL PROTECTION 132

From Ethology to Ethics, 132

Bioethics, Behavior, and Conflicting Values, 134

Farm Animal Ethology and Bioethics, 137

Notes, 139

CONCLUSIONS 141

ABOUT THE AUTHOR 151

REFERENCES 153

BIBLIOGRAPHY 159

INDEX 161

FOREWORD

Shortly after reading the manuscript for this book, I happened to see a photograph of a huge sow nursing her piglets. The caption of the picture, "A Moment of Bliss," at first seemed ridiculous to me. Then I realized that it was justified if the photographer really believed that he could read the human equivalent of ecstasy on the face and in the attitude of the sow. In any case the picture put me in the mood to examine ethological concepts in the long perspective of the attempts made throughout prehistory and history to establish similarities between human behavior and animal behavior.

Man's age-old fascination with his kinship to animals is apparent in the oldest known pictorial representation of humankind, the so-called "sorcerer" in the Trois Frères Paleolithic cave. It shows a man dressed in the hide of an animal and wearing antlers as if to suggest some kind of link between the human and animal worlds. During historical times there has been a continuing tradition of legends, fables, and stories that certainly began before Aesop and that are still popular now—as shown by the success of Orwell's *Animal Farm,* Bach's *Jonathan Livingston Seagull,* and Walt Disney's film fantasies. The general theme is to illustrate points of behavior, morality, and wisdom through actions by animals.

Concepts in Ethology

Beginning with Christianity and throughout the Middle Ages, the compilers of bestiaries used animals, real or imaginary ones (think of the unicorn!), to illustrate Biblical teachings and to symbolize human attributes. The earliest bestiaries put emphasis on divine revelation in nature and on the conflicts between good and evil; then they became more secular. In the thirteenth century the beasts in the *Bestiaire d'Amour*, for example, served to illustrate the different kinds of behavior that men and women employ when engaged in the games of love. In the *Divine Comedy* Dante used specific animals to symbolize the epitome of certain passions, vices, and virtues. In *The Prince* Machiavelli allegorized the qualities required for political power, using in particular the lion and the fox because strength and guile are both required for achieving supremacy.

Thus, it has long been a practice among human beings to identify most of their own behavioral traits with those of one or another of the different animal species. Even intelligence, sense of freedom, moral qualities, and political propensities have been so personified. Conversely, most aspects of animal behavior have been described in human terms, each animal species being discussed as if its way of dealing with the problems of its own life involved attitudes borrowed from the human repertoire. Julian Huxley himself designated the social signals used by animals in attack and defense as forms of "ritualization"—a word obviously loaded with anthropomorphic cultural values. But in all these comparisons until our times man regarded himself, in Hamlet's words, as "the paragon of animals," possessing to a higher degree than any other animal the attributes judged most desirable.

Recently, however, a different trend has appeared in the comparative evaluation of men and beasts. The new fashion, based on a misreading of scientific knowledge, is to affirm that the genes we have inherited from our animal precursors have determined once and for all our behavioral patterns,

Foreword

especially the most unpleasant of them. Many contemporary writers seem to find it more to their taste, unless it be simply more remunerative, to discourse about the "territorial imperative" and the "naked ape" than to account for the spontaneously gentle and altruistic behavior commonly observed among primitive people or for the conscious efforts that many sophisticated people make to overcome their bestial tendencies.

In my opinion it is no longer necessary to point out that we are closely related to the higher primates by our bodily structure (including our brain) and by our physiological and psychological attributes (including our instinctive reactions). What is acutely needed, however, is an emphasis on the fact that what makes us human is not what we are biologically but what we do with our biological endowment. Common sense shows that being human means supplementing or even replacing altogether the unconscious instinctive reactions of our animal nature by conscious, goal-directed responses.

In the "Conclusions" section of his monograph Professor Fox makes clear the limitations and the dangers of applying the results of animal studies to the problems of human behavior. The difficulty comes from the fact that, whereas much is known concerning man as an animal, hardly anything is known scientifically concerning what is uniquely human about human nature. I am reminded here of the remarks made by a German philosopher at the turn of the century. When asked to state what he thought of the sciences of man in his time, he replied, "In my young days we used to ask ourselves anxiously, 'What *is* man?' Now scientists seem to be satisfied with the answer that he *was* an ape." And yet knowing that we have evolved from animals is clearly not sufficient to explain why and how we differ so profoundly from even our closest animal relatives, the higher apes, in our behavior and in our social structures. Fortunately, there are indications that the ethological approach may eventually help to

Concepts in Ethology

define the forces that have been at work for more than a million years in differentiating *Homo sapiens* from the rest of the animal kingdom.

Ethologists try to recognize and define in detail the distinctive behavioral traits exhibited by a particular population when observed in its own natural habitat. This approach is qualitatively different from that of experimental psychologists who aim at conditioning the behavior of beasts or men by the use of either punishment or reward—who aim in other words at artificially changing behavior.

Professor Fox richly demonstrates in his monograph that all kinds of animals living normally in their natural habitats exhibit patterns of behavior distinctive for each phase of their development; these behavior patterns give to each population a social identity transcending its obvious biological characteristics. Species which are closely related in evolutionary descent commonly show profound differences in social organization and behavior. And, conversely, species which are biologically very different may display striking social similarities. I shall illustrate this dissociation between anatomical and social evolution by using examples taken largely from Professor Fox's own studies. These examples deal with three species of canids—the red fox, the coyote, and the wolf—which exhibit contrasting types of social behavior despite their anatomical and physiological similarities.

Most individual foxes lead a solitary life. The male and the female come together only for a short time during the breeding season; the cubs are deserted when they are around five months of age. In contrast, the male and the female coyote stay together beyond the breeding season and they drive their young from the home territory only when these reach about eleven months of age. Young wolves, however, usually stay with the parents, which themselves are pair-bonded; the pack represents an extended family consisting of the mother, the offspring, a male leader (which may or may

Foreword

not be the father), one or two other adults, and subadults from an earlier litter. In passing, it is of interest that different races of wolves exhibit specialization within this highly organized social pattern. In Canada, for example, there is a race of wolves that exists in small packs and specializes in hunting deer, and there is another race that travels in larger packs and preys on moose.

Not only do foxes, coyotes, and wolves differ in social organization but their social differences are correlated with differences in temperament between the individual animals of each litter within a given species. Typically, a litter of red foxes is homogeneous, all the cubs being extremely aggressive, assertive, and exploratory. In contrast, the individual cubs in a litter of wolves differ markedly from each other; some are outgoing and aggressive, and others are extremely timid. Such individual differences seem to be related to the fact that foxes are solitary animals and therefore must be able very early to fend for themselves, whereas wolves function as a complex hunting pack in which individual animals have different roles.

Such ethological observations can of course be analyzed in terms of genetic and environmental determinism. But it may be more useful to speculate, as Professor Fox does, on their relevance to human affairs. Biologically, human beings are of course much closer to higher primates than to wolves—yet human beings display remarkable similarities to wolves in their social evolution and in their relation to the environment and differ greatly in these respects from the higher primates. The size of the hunting area required by bands of human hunters and gatherers is of the same order as that required by wolf packs—between fifty and a hundred square miles per individual man or wolf. In contrast, bands of herbivorous baboons and gorillas need only two or three square miles per head. The fact that cooperative hunting requires an extensive home range may be related to the ten-

Concepts in Ethology

dency of men and wolves to wander, in contrast to the sedentary habits of baboons and gorillas. The human longing for the "open road" does not seem to be in the "naked ape" or "territorial imperative" tradition.

It is certain that ethological studies of animals can make a contribution to the understanding of human behavior and social organization by suggesting homologies and analogies that transcend obvious biological determinism. For example, the complex psychological repertoire associated with human mother love did not spring into being with *Homo sapiens*; suckling is clearly homologous in man and apes. In fact, this repertoire has much deeper evolutionary origins. Niko Tinbergen once wittily remarked that when human beings marvel at the care displayed by a mouse nursing her young and exclaim, "How human mice are!" they ought to say instead, "Aren't human beings exactly like mice!" Professor Fox discusses many other examples in which ideas about the present problems of humankind can be derived from studies of the effects exerted on animals by factors such as releasers and inhibitors, early influences, crowding or isolation, enriched or impoverished environments, and domestication as one aspect of civilization.

But while human beings share with animals a vast repertoire of instincts and have in common with them many responses to environmental stimuli, it is also true that they are much freer than are animals from the tyranny of their biological inheritance—the reason being that the principal modality of human evolution has been psychosocial rather than genetic for more than a thousand centuries. Human beings are not slaves of their hormones and genes; they can exercise moral judgment if they want. Instead of reacting mechanically to the forces of nature, they function in a world of symbols, purposive actions, and creative ideals.

This does not mean that human beings are not influenced by their environment. In many respects they react to it and

Foreword

are shaped by it in a rather stereotyped manner, just as animals are, but they commonly refuse to remain where the accidents of life have placed them and furthermore they rarely submit passively to environmental influences. It is interesting to note, for example, that after centuries of residence in Abyssinia, southern India, or China, some Jewish communities have retained their own cultures, even though they now look like their African, Indian, and Chinese neighbors—evidence that social traditions, which are the most distinctive aspects of human life, can be more persistent than biological inheritance. Most human beings search deliberately for conditions that help them to achieve what they want to do and to become what they want to be. They even create such conditions if these do not exist in their surroundings.

Furthermore, human beings are not prisoners of the evolutionary trends—biological and social—in which they find themselves. Individually and collectively, they are capable of changing not only their physical environments but also their life-styles. Human societies have been known to retrace their steps and to change the course of their social evolution in order to start new ways of life based on different sets of values. There is no evidence that an animal society can develop—let alone tolerate—a counterculture advocating a new social organization or way of life. But countercultures have been the most significant forces in determining the course of human societies and bringing about the renewal of civilizations.

Although it is unjustified to extrapolate broadly from animal studies to human behavior, there was a basis of truth in the imaginings of the medieval compilers of bestiaries who used animals to symbolize human attitudes, feelings, and actions. Looking through the whole animal world, it is possible to find almost any characteristic we need to explain human behavior at a given time in a given place. Animal societies provide many examples of aggressiveness and territorial imperative, but they also provide examples of altruism and cooperation—for care of the young, food storage, protection against predators, and maintenance of territory by harmless signals. And so it goes for almost any set of opposite and complementary behavioral traits we can imagine. Such traits can always be found somewhere in the animal kingdom, and all of them exist in the human species; the fact that they exist in a potential state does not mean that they need be expressed in reality.

Experience shows that human societies can exist in very different forms. Within a given geographical region all the land may be held in common, or a few people may own huge estates while many others have no personal property at all; the political structure may be monarchy by divine right, or it may be aristocratic, democratic, or essentially anarchic in form; some populations are sedentary and others tend to wander; some societies exalt altruism and others are based on selfishness, and so forth. The biological basis for each and every one of these social characteristics exists potentially in all human beings and can be recognized in many animals. For each of the characteristics which account for our bestiality there is somewhere in the animal kingdom an opposite one which accounts for our humanity. The more important point, however, is that human beings can *choose* between bestiality and humanity. They have long been and continue to be engaged in a struggle between the beast and the angel that reside in them.

Environmental and social circumstances unquestionably influence which of the characteristics present in human nature are allowed to predominate. But in the final analysis the selection involves personal choices and the willingness to make decisions. This matter of choice and decision helps in defining the relevance of ethological concepts to human life. Darwin's book *The Expression of the Emotions in Man and*

Foreword

Animals provided some evidence that the scientific methods of ethology can be applied to human beings. Scientists have tended to neglect this field of research, but a few investigators have recently revived it, especially with regard to body language, facial expressions, social conventions, and ritualistic responses to stimuli. Even though limited, their findings strongly suggest that much of human behavior has a long evolutionary background and that some of its determinants are genetically derived.

Genes, however, do not determine traits; they only control the emergence of the phenotype. Behavior being the phenotypic expression of genes, the fundamental and unresolved problem is to understand how each particular human being, and each particular social group, elects to emphasize some aspects of the behavioral repertoire of *Homo sapiens* and to repress others—a process which obviously involves choices and the exercise of free will. Ethological observations can help in defining the potentialities and the limits that determine the range of behavioral expression, but they cannot predict what choices and decisions a particular animal or person will make in a particular situation at a particular time.

As far as can be judged, living things differ quantitatively with regard to their degree of freedom from environmental and social constraints, and this is perhaps the origin of their qualitative differences. Modern man still believes that he has greater latitude than other animals with regard to environmental and social constraints and this is why—although he seems to enjoy reading publications about the territorial and other imperatives of the naked ape—he still considers himself the paragon of animals.

René Dubos

The Rockefeller University
March 1974

INTRODUCTION TO SECOND EDITION

The hiatus of over 20 years in coming out with a second, revised edition of this book is a time span that I believe cannot be filled simply by including an updated, annotated review of some of the concepts in ethology that have waxed and waned during this interval. Since the influence of sociobiology and computer simulation in the late 1970s, I found classical or basic ethology being perverted by mechanistic reductionism and determinism. I found it intensely boring also, especially after my first taste of field ethology studying the whistling dholes or wild dogs in the Indian jungle. Rather than simply adding some new concepts and findings about animal and human behavior to update this reissue of my book, I have chosen instead to emphasize how ethology has become an integral part of animal welfare science and bioethics, since it provides an objective way of determining animal well-being. Ethology has come to play an increasingly important role in animal care or husbandry, in setting animal care/welfare standards, and in enhancing the human-animal bond. An understanding of ethology makes a qualitative difference in human-animal relationships and provides a scientific basis for the bioethical principles of animal welfare and protection. I was greatly encouraged during the 1980s when more ethologists began to focus on endangered species' environmental needs, their social ecology and *telos* or purpose in ecosystem maintenance, and on the care of wild animals in captivity.[1]

Many seemed to pick up on some of the issues that I raised in the first edition of this book, *Concepts in Ethology: Animal and Human Behavior*. I have been heartened by the fact that the British Veterinary Ethology Society, which I helped found in the 1970s, became the International Association for Applied Animal Ethology in the 1990s, with members doing ethological studies focusing on animal well-being and tackling a variety of animal welfare concerns. There are now university chairs in animal welfare science, and veterinary colleges in many countries have included ethology in the undergraduate teaching curriculum and offer graduate and diploma courses.

Classical ethology has overcome the trends of reductionism and reification by focusing on cognitive ethology. This is in large part due to a colleague of the late Rene Dubos (who wrote the Foreword for the first edition) at The Rockefeller University, namely, Professor Donald Griffin. Griffin's then-controversial book published in 1977, entitled *The Question of Animal Awareness*, helped turn the tide. Harvard Professor E. O. Wilson, who set off the sociobiology craze in the early 1970s, redeemed himself in my eyes in 1984 when he published his book *Biophilia*. I was concerned then that ethologists and ecologists were pursuing their research studies with little concern for animal welfare and conservation, since the majority were silent on these issues.

Advances in applied animal ethology, especially in the vet-

Introduction to Second Edition

erinary field, were spearheaded during the late 1970s by my friend Dr. Andrew Fraser, editor of the scientific journal *Applied Animal Ethology*. Like Dr. Fraser, also a veterinarian, I became deeply involved in such questions as animal awareness, pain perception, animal well-being, animal welfare, animal rights, and human-animal relationships.

Dr. Fraser anticipated me in bringing bioethics into the scope of veterinary practice and animal husbandry and inspired me to incorporate bioethics in this second edition of my book since ethics is a natural component of human ethology. Since ethics and moral codes influence how humans behave, relate to each other, and treat animals, human ethology must inevitably look at the bioethical basis of human behavior.

So after teaching ethology (from 1967 to 1976) at Washington University, St. Louis, I decided to more directly investigate human-animal relationships and bioethics as Scientific Director of The Humane Society of the United States. I had to confront the ethics, or the lack thereof, of keeping animals in zoos, trapping and hunting them, experimenting upon and domesticating them, and also raising them intensively in the confines of factory farms. This confrontation necessitated close encounters with the industries and persons involved in such animal use and abuse, and an opportunity to study people's attitudes, values and behavior toward various animal species. In the process I had to explore religions, anthropology, mythology, and other fields to find the origins of people's attitudes and values toward animals. My findings are detailed in my recent book *The Boundless Circle: Caring for Creatures and Creation*,[2] and earlier in my book *Inhumane Society: The American Way of Exploiting Animals*.[3]

I also applied various concepts in ethology to the care and welfare assessment of laboratory[4] and farm animals.[5]

Concepts in Ethology

In order to improve the ethological understanding of animals, which is a prerequisite to their optimal care and well-being, I first had to gain acceptance especially in the biomedical research and farm animal production science circles, that ethology was an objective, scientific discipline, and the best way to study animals' subjective states, emotional reactions, social relations, and psychological needs. Applying ethological principles to the care and handling of these animals could help make farm animals healthier and more productive, and lead to more reliable conclusions from laboratory animal experiments. People involved in vivisection and factory farming have continued to resist ethological considerations and the bioethical ramifications of keeping animals under conditions that deny them their basic behavioral needs.

I shall never forget the snickers of ridicule from a small group of American scientists reacting to what my friend the late Konrad Lorenz said at his opening address at an international gathering of ethologists in Rennes in 1974. He simply advised, "Before you can study an animal, you must first love it."

Lorenz was talking about intuition and empathic, rather than instrumental, knowledge that is derived from a love of one's subject—as any good artist would affirm. He was warning fellow ethologists not to follow the mechanistic path of scientific reductionism. The essence of ethology is holism—the study of whole organisms, their development, their environment, and their communities. This leads to an understanding of their *telos,* and by reflexion, raises the question of our relationships with organisms and our duties, if any, to not alter their *telos,* destroy their *ecos,* and harm their *ethos.*

One of my delights as an ethologist was exploring the ontogenetic and phylogenetic linkages of animals' (especially canids)[6] telos, ecos, and ethos. So I was shocked to hear some

Introduction to Second Edition

top scientists embarking on the new frontier of creating genetically engineered animals proclaim that the concept of animals' telos has no biological foundation and "belongs to the realm of mysticism . . . and we can't base sound public policy on mysticism."[7] I realized they sought to deny that animals have any intrinsic value, interests, ethos, and telos because they are dedicated to creating a bioindustrialized, artificial ecos, and directing the telos of all useful organisms toward serving the ecology of the industrial economy, rather than contributing to the sustainable economy of Nature's ecology.

This is where my interest in ethology and concern for animals led to an inquiry into people's perception of animals, and how culture and education influenced their appreciation and treatment of fellow beings. Ethics play a significant role in human behavior and influence our relationships with each other, with animals, and with the natural environment. But our ethics are only as good as our ethological and ecological understanding of human nature, of animals' needs and welfare, and of the dynamics and processes of ecosystems. This is why, following a review of the human-animal bond, which is an addition to this second edition, I discuss the bioethics of human relationships with animals and Nature.

Concepts in ethology have changed considerably since the first edition of this book, not simply because of the vast amount of research studies that have been done over the intervening twenty-plus years. With changing attitudes toward animals—that they are not unfeeling, instinct-driven automatons but have feelings, minds, interests, and intrinsic value—so concepts in ethology and the kinds of questions ethologists ask, have changed. The changes have been all for the good, I believe, especially in the study of animals' minds or so-called cognitive ethology. These new developments in ethology have been the subject of several books and symposia, the most groundbreaking of which I have included in a bibliography at the end of this revised edition.

Notes

1. (1984) *The Whistling Hunters: Field Studies of the Asiatic Wild Dog,* Cuon alpinus. Albany, NY: State University of New York Press.
2. (1996) Wheaton, IL: Quest Books.
3. (1990) New York: St. Martin's Press.
4. (1986) *Laboratory Animal Husbandry: Ethology, Welfare and Experimental Variables.* Albany, NY: State University of New York Press.
5. (1984) *Farm Animals: Husbandry, Behavior and Veterinary Practice.* Baltimore, MD: University Press.
6. (1980) *The Soul of the Wolf.* Boston, MA: Little, Brown & Co. Reprinted (1992) New York: Lyons and Burford.
7. (1992) *Superpigs and Wondercorn: The Brave New World of Biotechnology and Where It All May Lead.* New York: Lyons and Burford.

Books by Dr. Michael W. Fox

Eating with Conscience: The Bioethics of Food (1997) New Sage Press, Troutdale, Oregon
Concepts in Ethology: Animal Behavior and Bioethics (revised edition 1997) Krieger Publishing Co., Malabar, Florida
The Boundless Circle (1996) Quest Books, Wheaton, Illinois
Agricide: The Hidden Farm and Food Crisis That Affects Us All (revised edition 1996) Krieger Publishing Co., Malabar, Flordia
Super Pigs and Wonder Corn: The Brave New World of Biotechnology and Where It All Might Lead (1992) Lyons & Burford, New York
The Soul of the Wolf (reprint edition 1992) Lyons and Burford, New York
Understanding Your Dog (revised edition 1992) St. Martin's Press, New York
Understanding Your Cat (revised edition 1992) St. Martin's Press, New York
You Can Save the Animals (1991) St. Martin's Press, New York
Supercat (1991) Howell Books, New York
Superdog (1990) Howell Books, New York
Inhumane Society: The American Way of Exploiting Animals (1990) St. Martin's Press, New York
St. Francis of Assisi, Animals, and Nature (1989) Center for Respect of Life and Environment, Washington, D.C.
The New Eden (1989) Lotus Press, Santa Fe, New Mexico
The New Animal Doctor's Answer Book (1989) Newmarket Press, New York
Laboratory Animal Husbandry (1986) State University of New York Press, Albany
Between Animal and Man: The Key to the Kingdom (reprint edition 1986) Krieger Publishing Co., Malabar, Florida
The Dog: Its Domestication and Behavior (reprint edition 1987) Krieger Publishing Co., Malabar, Florida
The Whistling Hunters (1984) State University of New York Press, Albany
Behavior of Wolves, Dogs, and Related Canids (reprint edition 1984) Krieger Publishing Co., Malabar, Florida
One Earth, One Mind (reprint edition 1984) Krieger Publishing Co., Malabar, Florida
Farm Animals: Husbandry, Behavior and Veterinary Practice (1983) University Press, Baltimore, Maryland
The Healing Touch (1983) Newmarket Press, New York (paperback version of *Dr. Michael Fox's Massage Program for Cats and Dogs,* 1981, Newmarket Press, New York)
Love Is a Happy Cat (1982) Newmarket Press, New York
How to Be Your Pet's Best Friend (1981) Coward, McCann & Geoghegan, New York
Returning to Eden: Animal Rights and Human Responsibility (1980) Viking Press, New York
Understanding Your Pet (1978) Coward, McCann and Geoghegan, New York

Canine Behavior (reprint edition 1972) Charles C. Thomas Publishing, Springfield, Illinois
Integrative Development of Brain and Behavior in the Dog (1971) University of Chicago Press
Canine Pediatrics (1966) Charles C. Thomas Publishing, Springfield, Illinois

Editor of:

Advances in Animal Welfare Science (annual series 1984–1987) Martinus Nijhoff in Holland, and The Humane Society of the United States, Washington, D.C.
The Wild Canids (reprint edition 1983) Krieger Publishing Co., Malabar, Florida
On the Fifth Day: Animal Rights and Human Ethics (1977) Acropolis Press, Washington, D.C. (With R. K. Morris)
Readings in Ethology and Comparative Psychology (1973) Brooks/Cole, California
Abnormal Behavior in Animals (1968) Saunders, Philadelphia

Children's Books:

Animals Have Rights Too (1991) Crossroads/Continuum, New York
The Way of the Dolphin (1981) Acropolis Books, Washington, D.C.
The Touchlings (1981) Acropolis Books, Washington, D.C.
Lessons from Nature: Fox's Fables (1980) Acropolis, Washington, D.C.
Whitepaws: A Coyote-Dog (1979) Coward, McCann & Geoghegan, New York
Wild Dogs Three (1977) McCann & Geoghegan, New York
What Is Your Dog Saying? (1977) M. W. Fox and Wende Devlin Gates, Coward, McCann & Geoghegan, New York
What Is Your Cat Saying? (1977) M. W. Fox and Wende Devlin Gates, Coward, McCann & Geoghegan, New York
Ramu and Chennai* (1975) Coward, McCann & Geoghegan, New York
Sundance Coyote** (1974) Coward, McCann & Geoghegan, New York
The Wolf*** (1973) Coward, McCann & Geoghegan, New York
Vixie, The Story of a Little Fox (1973) Coward, McCann & Geoghegan, New York

*   Best Science Book Award, National Teachers' Association
**   Nominee for Mark Twain Awards
***   Christopher Award for children's literature

Concepts in Ethology

CHAPTER 1

ETHOLOGY—THE STUDY OF MAN AND BEAST

Ethology may be defined simply as the study of behavior. It differs radically from comparative experimental psychology by virtue of the fact that it deals with the adaptation of animals to their environment through genetic programming and evolutionary selection or as a consequence of experiences (including cultural experiences in man) during early life. Experimental psychology has suffered notoriously from reductionism and is hardly comparative when the work is limited primarily to rats, pigeons, and a few neurotic captive monkeys, but many of the experimental methods of the comparative psychologist, especially operant conditioning, are utilized by the ethologist. In this volume a number of important ethological concepts and phenomena have been selected for review to show the scope and potential of ethology and its relevance to animal and human medicine.

The Beginnings of Ethology

Ethology grew out of studies of the natural history of animals by Huxley, Darwin, and Fabre. In the United

NOTE: This chapter is based on a lecture in the Wesley W. Spink Lectures on Comparative Medicine presented at the University of Minnesota, St. Paul campus, on October 16, 1973.

Concepts in Ethology

States at the turn of the century Craig and Whitman made some classical ethological studies of pigeons, but on the whole the emerging science of ethology in the United States was overshadowed by behaviorism, a branch of psychology founded by Watson. In the last fifteen years or so, however, a distinct field of ethology has developed in the United States, initially under the leadership of T. C. Schneirla at the American Museum of Natural History and two of his students, Daniel S. Lehrman and Frank Beach.

In Europe ethology became an established science much earlier. In the 1930s Konrad Lorenz and Nikolaas Tinbergen started to make objective observations of animals in their natural habitats and to examine specific problems of animal behavior in the laboratory where the relevant variables could be controlled and appropriately manipulated. Many of Tinbergen's field observations were followed by experiments in the field and in the laboratory using certain models; these models, which are termed sign stimuli or releasers, will be discussed later. Tinbergen's approach, based on a premise put forward by Jakob von Uexküll, focused on the Umwelt or perceptual world of the animal under study. When Tinbergen moved to Oxford (where he founded the Department of Animal Behavior), one of his graduate students, Christian Baerends, continued the work in Holland. While Tinbergen studied the stimuli releasing, guiding, and organizing an animal's behavior and the complex organization of sequences of behavior, Lorenz, on the other hand, was concerned with the evolution and the development of behavior. He found that the evolution of behavior can be studied by examining and comparing the same or closely related species in different habitats and also by looking at different species that live in similar ecological niches and cope with similar environmental problems. In

Ethology—The Study of Man and Beast

Cambridge, England, W. H. Thorpe, a comparative psychologist in the true sense, established a subdepartment of animal behavior which is now directed by Robert Hinde. In the British and American schools of ethology field and laboratory studies are complementary.

Ethology today is interdisciplinary, using many of the concepts and techniques derived from genetics, ecology, endocrinology, and neurophysiology. A recent trend in ethology has been to revitalize the holistic gestalt principle of observing the individual and its social group and identifying the environmental determinants of group and individual behavior; this is related to the area of socioecology, which is discussed further in chapter 2. The relatively new area of human ethology holds much promise for the ethologist, the anthropologist, and the psychiatrist alike.

Applied Ethology

Ethology has much in common with the clinical method of direct observation in that the approach in both is at once etiological, phenomenological, and teleological. Because of its holistic and integrative orientation, ethology can also serve as a core discipline linking studies in areas such as veterinary medicine (Fox, 1967), agricultural science (Klinghammer and Fox, 1971), and (at the basic college science level) biology and psychology (Fox, 1973). In agricultural science, for example, ethology can add new dimensions to studies of animal handling and restraint, reproduction and maternal behavior, nutrition and grazing patterns, housing, spacing, and social grouping. In veterinary medicine courses in ethology can serve to integrate courses in physiology, anatomy, and biochemistry, so that the dynamics of the whole animal in relation to other animals and to its environment may be conceptualized. In clinical pathology a knowledge of behavior is essential where, for example, crowding stress may exacerbate disease. Certain relationships between individual animals in captivity or between a pet and its owner may be a cause of stress, infection, or psychosomatic disorder (discussed further in chapter 3). Similarly in human medicine ethology could offer the student a more holistic view of disease where social and environmental factors must be considered in addition to the behavior, role, and personality of the patient himself. Specific examples of abnormal behavior will be given in chapter 2 in order to show further how ethology can be applied to psychiatry and to comparative psychopathology in domestic and captive animals.

The balance of this section contains a review of some of the phenomena and concepts of ethology which are essential to a basic understanding of the science. It is anticipated that this material will also provide some stimulus for reflective introspection about human nature and in addition may open new doors of perception for people in other disciplines.

The first examples of ethological phenomena were derived from studies originated by Tinbergen, who used models to "turn on" or release the behavior of various animals. The releasing features of models that evoke particular behaviors are termed sign stimuli (Tinbergen, 1950). For example, a male stickleback develops a red breast during the breeding season. A crude oval model painted red underneath will be attacked violently if it is placed in the stickleback's tank (Figure 1). Similarly, an oval silver-colored model which only vaguely resembles the form of an egg-

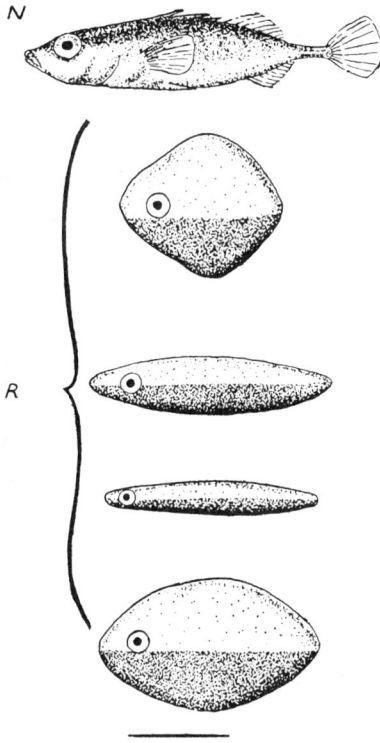

FIG. 1. A series of models (R) effective in releasing aggression in male sticklebacks. The models were painted red on the underside, but otherwise they did not resemble N, a scale model of the species, in shape or detail. (From Tinbergen, 1950.)

filled female stickleback will elicit courtship behavior rather than aggression from the male. The model need have no eyes or fins as long as it is more or less oval in shape and is of the correct color. It is interesting to note that the retinal receptors of the female stickleback change during the breeding season and become increasingly sensitive to red so that she will be attracted by the red breast of the male.

A newly hatched herring gull chick will peck at bright objects provided they are small and round; since its mother's bill has an orange-red spot near the tip, it will also peck there. This action of the chick stimulates the mother to regurgitate food and therefore is an important survival-promoting mechanism. Through the reinforcement or reward of receiving food the chick soon learns to peck preferentially at the mother's bill. The bill mark which releases, orients, and guides the pecking response of the young chick is a classic example of a sign stimulus. Tinbergen (1950) showed that a herring gull chick more readily pecks at a cardboard model that has a spot on it than at a model that has no distinct mark; furthermore, he discovered that the same chick will peck even more enthusiastically at a pencil that has black and white or red and white bands on it. A model that evokes more response than its natural prototype (in this case the bill of the chick's own mother) is referred to as a supranormal releaser. Another example of this is seen in many nesting birds such as the oyster catcher; if oyster catchers are presented with eggs that are more brightly speckled or are larger than

FIG. 2. An example of a supranormal releaser. An oyster catcher reacts to a giant egg in preference to its own egg (*foreground*) and a herring gull's egg (*left*). (From Tinbergen, 1950.)

Ethology—The Study of Man and Beast

their own, they will desert their nests in order to incubate the new eggs placed by the side of the nest (Figure 2).

Releasing stimuli are not exclusively visual. The female turkey with a brood of chicks apparently responds not to their sight but to their sound. (If she is deafened, she may ignore them or even kill them.) When a stuffed polecat fitted with wheels is pulled by a string (or moved by a small internal motor) toward the turkey, she will immediately attack it. If the stuffed model is equipped with a small tape recorder inside it which emits the "cheep-cheep" sound of turkey chicks, however, the hen will accept the model and allow it to move underneath her.

A number of butterflies and moths have symmetrical circles or eyespots on their underwings which they display when they are alarmed by a would-be predator such as a bird. Many of these insects contain substances that are toxic to birds, and the eyespots serve as aposematic or warning signals. Blest (1957) placed a mealworm on a board and marked identical symbols on each side of it. When he put a cross or a square on each side of the worm, one of his bird subjects would readily hop forward and eat it. If, however, he placed circles resembling eyespots on each side of the worm, the birds would avoid it. Many of these birds had already encountered eyespot butterflies that were poisonous, containing cardiac glycosides which made the birds sick. In order to discover whether the avoidance of eyespot butterflies was innate, Blest hand-raised a number of birds so that he could prevent their exposure to the poisonous butterflies. When the hand-raised birds were first offered a mealworm with eyespot symbols on each side, many of them did not approach the worm, implying that in some birds avoidance may indeed be innate.

FIG. 3. (*top*) Approach, investigation, and greeting of a model (a social releaser) by an eight-week-old pup. (*bottom*) The duration of interaction with the model is greatest during the fear period in pups at eight to ten weeks of age. At an earlier age hunger increases responsiveness. (From Fox, 1971b.)

Ethology—The Study of Man and Beast

In man an important social releaser is the smile, the development of which has been studied by a number of workers. The human infant that is two or three months old will smile at a very crude mask bearing a couple of eyespots. As the child's perception improves, however, smiling is released only by a more complete, human-looking mask; at this point the presence of a nose and a mouth becomes increasingly important in the gestalt of the releaser. A change occurs between seven and eight months of age when the child will not smile or will actually cry if it sees an unfamiliar mask (or an unfamiliar person). This marks what Spitz (1949) calls the onset of the anxiety period. A comparable fear period develops in the dog at about eight weeks of age (Figure 3).

Thorpe (1956) emphasizes that we should also consider the significance of acquired releasers in human behavior, since through operant or classical conditioning we learn to respond to certain elements in our environment as automatically as do animals whose responses are built into their instinctive repertoire. The releaser concept is also relevant in psychopathology in considering the potency of fetish objects—that is, where a particular object has a special symbolic meaning for an individual and releases certain affects which are not species typical (for example, the shoe fetish). Modern marketing research has recognized how important the releasing qualities of shape, color, size, and texture of various items are in attracting the consumer. Very orange oranges are more attractive than natural oranges (which are usually a mottled greenish yellow), and so oranges are dyed to increase their visual appeal. Packages, wrapping materials, and containers are made as visually attractive as possible in order to catch the shopper's eye. Hess (1965) found that when a person is looking at something he likes, the pupils of his eyes dilate; market researchers are now using the pupil response as an objective measure to determine the efficacy of television advertising and package designs. The ethics of such practices and of subliminal conditioning are questionable. In Western culture it is likely that the automobile is the ultimate supranormal releaser of all time. It provides many owners with a tangible means of expressing their personal status, sex, power, freedom, and independence.

DISPLACEMENT BEHAVIORS AND COMPROMISE POSTURES

Displacement behaviors are invariably correlated with some kind of conflict such as an approach-withdrawal conflict or some other conflicting pair of simultaneously aroused motivations such as flight and attack or, as in ducks and other birds, sexual attraction and territorial aggression. When two fighting cocks approach each other at the periphery of their territories, they immediately engage in aggressive but highly ambivalent behavior. They are torn between attacking and retreating because to approach further in order to attack would mean crossing into the other's territory. During such ambivalence various displacement behaviors have been observed, notably self-preening and ground-pecking.

Lorenz (1971) has shown that in ducks displacement preening and drinking actions have been incorporated into the temporal sequences of the courtship repertoire and have become inherited actions. During a courtship sequence the male duck approaches the female and at a certain proximity turns sideways, elevates the nearest wing, and begins to displacement preen. The action is the same as preening, but the amplitude and the intensity are different. In displacement preening the male exhibits his nuptial plumage, which serves to enhance the display considerably. In the second

Ethology—The Study of Man and Beast

kind of displacement activity ducks of some species lower their heads and grab a beakful of water which they swallow by elevating the head vertically; then they give a final flick of the beak to knock off any water droplets. Other species show this displacement drinking in a fragmented form: the duck lowers its head without taking in any water, raises its head as though to swallow, and finally flicks its beak as if there were water on it.

Displacement grooming and scratching are also very common in mammals under conditions of conflict or ambivalent motivation. When Doberman pinschers of certain lines are appropriately aroused, they turn around and start sucking their flanks. This displacement flank-sucking is analogous in its effect to the anxiety-relieving effects of thumb-sucking in infants. Displacement actions may therefore serve to de-arouse an animal that is in a state of conflict. Ekman and Friesen (1969) refer to similar displacement activities in man (scratching the scalp, wiping the nose or the eye, stroking the arm or the knee, or adjusting clothing) as self-adaptors; these are all self-directed displacement behaviors that occur during situations that cause minor tension, anxiety, or conflict.

The displacement eating and drinking that have been so well documented in birds and animals are also seen in man, especially at cocktail parties and receptions. Everyone tends to be a little anxious about his self-image and so on at first, but as soon as nibbling and sipping begin, conversations start to flow much more easily. It would seem that eating and drinking per se may facilitate interaction in a group while they serve as de-arousing facilitators at the same time. (Perhaps it is the more inhibited people who consequently engage in more displacement drinking and who ultimately have to be carried home!) The fact that deep-seated anxiety invariably underlies obesity and alcoholism tends to support the notion that oral gratification under emotionally stressful circumstances may temporarily alleviate anxiety and effect de-arousal. A vicious circle develops when the displacement activity itself is rewarding.

Another important category of actions has been classified as compromise postures (Tinbergen, 1950). For example, an animal may assume a posture which is a frozen attitude of two conflicting tendencies, principally the tendencies to approach and to withdraw or to attack and to flee. Such compromise movements, which like displacements are indicative of ambivalent motivations, have become highly ritualized in birds and are inherent components of courtship rituals. The albatross during courtship stretches its head upward and extends its wings outward; the position of the head represents the bird's inclination to fly away while the wings suggest its readiness to attack. These two action patterns combine to form a new and highly ritualized pattern associated with courtship display. Comparable ambivalence and compromise postures are exhibited by humans in social situations. The angle of the body and the head, the direction in which the body leans, and whether the attitude is "open" or "closed" are all indicative of such ambivalence. For instance, a shy person may sit with his arms folded (in a closed position), his trunk inclined backward, and his shoulders twisted away to one side during an interview.

A fascinating compromise movement is seen in ground-nesting birds when they are approached by a predator. These birds have evolved a distraction display in which the individual feigns a broken wing. Analysis reveals that the side of the bird on which the wing is "broken" (the side that is being dragged) is the side that is motivated to stay

FIG. 4. Courtship actions in the blue-footed booby. (*top*) The female foot-treads on a rock and the male approaches. He then gives a ritualized courtship display which combines the elements of flight and attack. (*bottom*) Subsequently the male pecks at and picks up twigs (possibly a displacement action or redirected aggression). Finally, the partners engage in reciprocal twig-giving. This may be incipient nest-building behavior or a derived form of ritualized feeding.

on the nest while the other side (the wing that is being flapped) is motivated to fly away. Similar compromise movements occur during courtship in the Burmese jungle fowl. As the male approaches the female, the side of the body closest to the female shows a tendency for withdrawal while the side farthest away shows a tendency to approach. The outside leg crosses over the inside leg, and the inside wing is drooped and dragged in a stylized "waltz." (A

FIG. 5. Some examples of derived infantile actions in adult animals and their behavioral origins. Inguinal or groin presentation is a social gesture of adult canids, as illustrated by an adult gray fox, coyote-dog hybrids, and a wolf. (*facing page, top*) A pup remains passive to allow the mother to clean it; it displays a similar response when it is touched by another pup during play. (*facing page, bottom*) Mobbing of the mother by wolf cubs to cause her to regurgitate food; greeting and mobbing of the pack leader by adult wolves.

sequence of courtship actions in the blue-footed booby is shown in Figure 4.)

DERIVED ACTIVITIES

Derived activities are those actions which can occur in motivational contexts other than those in which they are usually seen. Infantile food-begging actions may reappear in adults as signals of appeasement or submission (Figure 5), and some actions associated with sexual behavior occur in aggressive contexts. These may be referred to respectively as socioinfantile and sociosexual actions.

Socioinfantile derived activities in primates occur especially during courtship as submissive appeasement gestures; the female assumes a submissive posture and at the same time may solicit grooming. In some courting birds the female displays a completely infantile food-begging posture, and the male, before consummating the sexual act, feeds her (a lizard, if they are roadrunners, or a fish, if they are terns). Such infantile behavior may serve to remotivate a potentially aggressive male. In adult wolves infantile food-soliciting actions are directed toward the pack leader and are identical to the actions of cubs while they are being cleaned and fed by their parents. (Infantile behavior in wolves is discussed further in chapter 2.) Psychoanalytic descriptions (rather than interpretations) of regression in man show that this phenomenon is closely analogous to what ethologists refer to as socioinfantile behavior in animals. Solicitous submissive behavior is adaptive in many social situations for man and animal alike.

Socioinfantile behavior in animals appears to be related to altruism. A number of naturalists have found crippled adult birds (for instance, pelicans) which are unable to fend for themselves and yet are in good health. By assuming infantile food-soliciting postures they automatically release care-giving and feeding behavior in other adults and so may be supported by their companions for several years under appropriate contingencies of reinforcement. A hand-raised bird as an adult may still assume an infantile food-begging posture when its caretaker approaches. Similar reinforcement of infantile behavior and dependency is also a factor in the way in which certain people raise and relate to pet dogs and children alike.

The second category of derived activities includes sociosexual behavior patterns. Wickler (1972) has studied these in detail in many animals. A classic example is the "penis dueling" which has become built into the aggressive display of squirrel monkeys. When two male squirrel monkeys approach each other, they become highly aroused and each has a penile erection. It would seem that the one to lose his erection first is the subordinate. Both male and female monkeys of many species will bow down and present the buttocks to a superior; this is not sexual presentation for copulation but a signal of submission. In these two examples behaviors primarily related to sexual activities have become emancipated and ritualized and occur as derived activities in very different social contexts. In one baboon species the male develops swollen red buttocks that mimic the hindquarters of an estrus female, the display serving to enhance signals of submission and appeasement. A casual

Ethology—The Study of Man and Beast

observer of a group of captive baboons might think that they are hypersexed because so much sexual presenting, mounting, and pelvic thrusting goes on, but much of this is sociosexual behavior; the apparently sexual presentation of the buttocks by either a male or a female is a sign of submission, and the dominant one reaffirms his or her status by mounting and making a few pelvic thrusts without intromission. In another example of sociosexual behavior a male may mount a female and give a direct stare to another male in order to put him down.

BODY LANGUAGE AND METACOMMUNICATION

Many of the threat gestures, submissive postures, and friendly intention movements of *Homo sapiens* are identical to those described in the higher primates. These include furrowing the brow, lowering the head, raising the shoulders, clenching the fists, puckering the mouth in an aggressive display, drooping the shoulders, looking away, lowering the head to one side, and retracting the lips horizontally in submission (Eibl-Eibesfeldt, 1972). The evolution of facial displays will be discussed further in chapter 2.

Analysis of behavior necessarily focuses upon the situation or the context in which the behavior occurs, and there is a strong interest today in metacommunication (Bekoff, 1973). A baboon, for example, is not simply a bundle of innate or instinctual responses. As a consequence of experience, socialization, and learning, it knows about its social group and learns to anticipate certain events in specific contexts. Furthermore, since baboons go into social situations with learned expectations, it is clear that the concepts of mood, role, and expectation are not relevant solely to human social behavior. This might be regarded critically as an anthropomorphism, but recent work with

FIG. 6. Play behavior in which threats and fighting are simulated exemplifies the phenomenon of metacommunication. (*top*) Two elephants, both aware that this is a "play" situation, engage in a stick game and then (*bottom*) in mock fighting.

primates and also with wolves increasingly supports the belief that animals are very much aware of each other as individuals, that metacommunication involving signals and context takes place, and that animals are indeed cognizant of different social contexts (Figure 6).

It is surprising that since Darwin's book *The Expression of the Emotions in Man and Animals* there have been very few studies of human ethology. Recently, however, there has been a revitalization of interest in this area. Investigators such as Eibl-Eibesfeldt (1970) in Germany and Birdwhistell (1970), Duncan (1969), and Mehrabian (1969) in the United States have been looking at various modes of human

Ethology—The Study of Man and Beast

communication—body language, postures, movements or kinesics, and rituals—and have been studying their developmental origins and pan-cultural similarities. We should also mention the work of Hall (1969), who shows that cultural differences in proximics or social spacing patterns (Figure 7) can affect communication between individuals of different backgrounds.

FIG. 7. When birds and animals settle, they space themselves out, a behavior reflecting the concept of social distance or proximity tolerance.

In South America, for example, normal everyday transactions between people occur regularly at a distance of about 1½ feet. This is within intimate distance for a North American who normally engages in day-to-day transactions at a distance of 2½ or 3 feet. When we put South Americans and North Americans together, the North American subjectively feels overwhelmed by the South American or decides that the latter is perhaps overly friendly, whereas the South American feels that the North American is distant and hard-to-reach, if not downright aloof! Such differences might be attributable to different modes of child-rearing, but the causes are yet to be determined. Both Hall and Sommer (1969) discuss how the design of offices, hospitals, and apartments also affects human behavior. As shown by Ekman and Friesen (1969), human ethology has clinical significance in addition; the body language of a patient can be "read" and used to measure attempts to deceive the therapist or the interviewer and to detect partially concealed states of conflict and anxiety.

CHEMICAL COMMUNICATION

Recently there has been an increased interest in the role of odors and chemical substances termed exhormones or pheromones in communication in connection with the social organization of animals (Gleason and Reynierse, 1969). It has been found that if a female mouse is inseminated and then immediately is exposed to a strange male (or to his urine or preputial gland material), she will not conceive. This pregnancy-blocking phenomenon is termed the Bruce effect. Although it may be difficult to demonstrate this in highly inbred mice (Marsden and Bronson, 1964), it is easily elicited in wild house mice and in deer mice. It seems that in nature this may have an important regulating

Ethology—The Study of Man and Beast

function, especially in dense populations where the probability of a recently inseminated female meeting a strange male would be increased. If, however, the olfactory tracts of the female have been severed before insemination, she will conceive normally despite the subsequent exposure to a strange male.

Two other phenomena of this sort—the Lee-Boot effect and the Whitten effect—have been observed in mice. When female mice are housed together, they have a social endocrine effect on each other that tends to prolong the estrus cycle (the Lee-Boot effect). When a male is placed among them, there is suddenly a synchrony of estrus four days later (the Whitten effect). Recently it has been shown that a synchrony of menstruation tends to develop among women living in dormitories. It is possible that this may eventually be linked to the presence of an external pheromone.

We are only beginning to understand the importance of pheromones in communication, social organization, endocrine function, and territorial spacing among animals. This is partly attributable to the relative lack of olfactory communication in human behavior, although Hall (1969) does point out certain cultures that rely a great deal on olfaction. It is possible that the extensive use of deodorants in some cultures may be an adaptation to reduce the effects of crowding stress.

Recently it has been discovered that a metabolite of testosterone in boars passes from the testes through the bloodstream into the parotid salivary glands. When a boar approaches a female and becomes sexually aroused, he salivates profusely and the pheromone in his saliva causes sexual arousal in the female. This substance has been isolated; when it is sprayed around the nasal region of the female, she will stand and present herself.

Michael, working in England, has been studying vaginal pheromones in rhesus monkeys and has shown that the constituents are virtually identical to extracts taken from the vagina of human females, from chimpanzees, and from baboons. Although our culture has taken us away from using our sense of smell, pheromones may still be operating at the level of the unconscious to modify subtly our emotions and behavior. Michael has demonstrated that if the nostrils of a male rhesus monkey are plugged up tightly with cotton wool, he will show no interest whatsoever in a receptive female. His sexual behavior and his erection seem to be totally dependent upon receiving an olfactory signal from the vagina of the female (Michael and Keverne, 1970).

SPACE AND TERRITORY

The use of space and the significance of territory are also important factors in the social behavior of animals. Animals such as lemmings have a high proximity intolerance for each other and are normally spaced out widely in their habitat. Proximity intolerance serves to ensure optimal utilization of available food sources and also to regulate the population. Those animals that do not possess territory or that are subordinate and are unable to hold territory are forced to emigrate. Where escape or emigration is not possible, such individuals succumb to crowding stress even when food is plentiful; their adrenal glands hypertrophy and eventually they develop Selye's stress syndrome. In many species of rodents infertility, agalactia, and reduction in the production of spermatozoa have been reported as well as increased susceptibility to infections and parasitic infestations.

It is generally found that an animal on its own territory is dominant but that when it is in a stranger's territory it is subordinate. Territoriality, therefore, not only

FIG. 8. Schema of physical and psychological spaces in an animal's world. The animal's home range is the total area it frequents, while its territory is that area which it defends. When the animal permits its mate or its owner to enter the critical distance zone, it will allow contact in the social and personal zones. A wild animal will flee if a person enters its flight distance zone, but it may attack if the intruder enters the critical distance zone.

spaces animals out but ensures, by virtue of the relative dominance of ownership, that an animal on its own ground is safe. This principle is utilized by the lion tamer: the ring is his territory, and consequently the lions are subordinate and easier to control.

Two other factors having to do with space have been described by Hediger (1950) as flight distance and critical distance (Figure 8). When a person encounters deer in the woods some distance away, they simply look at him, then turn away and continue grazing. If he attempts to move closer to them, at a certain distance they will retreat. He has crossed an invisible barrier into the flight distance zone. The second threshold is the boundary of the critical distance zone. If an animal is unable to escape and a person continues to move closer and closer to it, at a certain distance the animal may turn around and threaten the intruder and perhaps even attack him. The lion tamer always keeps within the flight distance of the cats so that they are literally pushed away from him by their own fear. If he accidentally steps within the critical distance, he may be attacked. If, however, he is able to touch a lion and to put his head into its mouth, it is because he has succeeded in socializing the animal to the extent that it permits him to enter within the social and intimate distance.

In connection with the flight distance reaction in humans Sommer (1969) reports that schizophrenic people often feel an intense aversion for proximity. They feel that a person close to them is literally standing inside them. This may be not only a breakdown or dissolution of body image but may also be related to the reactivation of a primitive flight distance response. The patient should be given the opportunity to seek a safe corner and to avoid stressful proximity anxiety. Recently it has been shown that convicts who have been diagnosed as psychopaths have a much higher proximity intolerance than normal people do. They begin to feel an intense anxiety and a need to strike out or to withdraw when another person approaches within three or four feet of them. More studies are needed on cultural differences in proximic patients and on abnormalities related to proximity intolerance.

Conclusions

It seems an insurmountable task to get into an animal's

Ethology—The Study of Man and Beast

consciousness and to discover what he is aware of and whether or not he is reflectively aware or purposefully knowing. Is man the only species who knows that he knows? Through the use of the models and releasers described earlier and by looking at how an animal relates to conspecifics, we are able to study some aspects of an animal's consciousness or awareness. An animal, rather like a preverbal child, can tell us quite a lot about what it is feeling through its displays and through its body language.

Part of the difficulty in getting into an animal's Umwelt is related to our own ability to project or to imagine. Given the limitations of our sensory apparatus and awareness, it is not a simple task to design appropriate experiments to explore, for example, the olfactory or chemical world of various species or to look into ultrasonic communication, animal sonar, and animal navigation. Advances in modern technology have helped considerably in this regard. Psychedelic drugs have enabled certain psychiatrists to expand their awareness and to cross the threshold into the perceptual world of mystics and schizophrenics. Ethologists sometimes cross the same threshold with animals by living with them and by subjectively becoming "at one" with them. Some contend that this initial link is essential for subsequent objective study.

Many anecdotes from the field and a few well-documented field observations provide us with examples of extraordinary feats and abilities of nonhuman animals which tend to indicate that there is not such a marked separation between man and animal as was once thought; rather, as in Teilhard de Chardin's (1971) sense, there is a continuum between animal and man. They differ mainly in the degree of cerebral complexity and social consciousness. Instances of altruism, for example, have been reported in dolphins, which have been known to support a sick member of the group at the surface of the water in order to breathe while others keep sharks at bay. Drowning swimmers have occasionally been rescued in this way by dolphins. Roger Payne has made a recording* of singing humpback whales; some of the songs last twenty or thirty minutes and are repeated with great accuracy and consistency and with subtle variations. Perhaps there is something more in these songs than in the stereotypic territorial singing of birds. Other workers have reported insightful behavior and cultural traditions in chimpanzees. They have observed, for instance, that chimpanzees strip twigs and probe them into a termite mound in search of insects and crush leaves to make a sponge for extracting water from the crevices of a tree; the tool-using techniques are handed down from parent to infant. This is indeed a high level of behavior, but it still seems to be a long way off from the complex technology of our own species.

When, however, we think about the hunting and gathering cultures, we are impressed by their lack of technology; in our own ethnocentric judgment such cultures might be described as primitive and we would naturally tend to say the same thing about chimpanzees and dolphins. But, looking at the matter in another way, one could say that the dolphins, for example, are so superbly adapted to their environment that they literally need no technology. The same is true of whales. Perhaps instead of spending millennia evolving technology as we have, they have spent their evolutionary time developing a consciousness and a communication system far more sophisticated than our own.

It is possible that the environment in which some

* *Songs of the Humpback Whale* (CRM Records, Del Mar, California).

Ethology—The Study of Man and Beast

animals live does not provide the challenge or the necessary reinforcement for the development of certain capacities which remain latent in these animals. A good example is tool-using in chimpanzees. In the wild most chimpanzees do not have to resort to tools, but in the laboratory they suddenly learn how to stack up boxes to make a ladder and to put poles together to make a long stick in order to reach food. Premack (1971) has recently taught a chimpanzee, Sarah, to read and write, while the Gardners (1969) have taught sign language to Washoe, another chimpanzee, who now has a vocabulary of over 140 words. The Gardners hope that they will be able to train more chimps to do this and that the chimps in turn may teach their offspring; if the experiment is successful, the result will be a new subspecies that utilizes observational learning and that is capable of transmitting culturally a newly acquired set of behaviors. The studies of Premack and the Gardners make it evident that although certain latent capabilities of animals have not been tapped in their natural environment, these capabilities can be brought out in the laboratory. Similarly, we have not yet fully explored the limits of human consciousness. From time immemorial man has sought mystical or "oceanic" experiences by various means including the use of drugs, chanting, and meditation (White, 1972). The intrapsychic processes involved in such altered states of consciousness remain a mystery in both animals and man. We must preserve a sense of wonder and not reduce animals to sets of neurons and automatic responses which can be predicted and controlled. If we keep our minds open to a wide range of new possibilities, disciplined and unbiased inquiry will be fruitful.

CHAPTER 2

THE BEHAVIOR OF WOLVES, DOGS, AND MAN

In this section I am going to discuss some of my own work on the comparative and developmental ethology of wild canids including the wolf, the coyote, and the red fox. The behavior of these wild canids will then be compared with the behavior of the domesticated dog in order to identify basic behavioral changes that have resulted from ten thousand years of selective breeding.

Three types of canids can be identified on the basis of certain characteristics in their social behavior (Fox, 1974). The Type 1 pattern is exemplified by the red fox. Except during the breeding season, most individual foxes lead a solitary life. The male and the female come together for a short time during the breeding season, and occasionally the male will assist the female in raising the cubs. The cubs are deserted at around five months of age. The Type 2 pattern is represented by the coyote, which usually maintains a permanent pair-bond independent of the breeding season. The male and the female stay together and share the same

NOTE: This chapter is based on a lecture in the Wesley W. Spink Lectures on Comparative Medicine presented at Carleton College in Northfield, Minnesota, on October 15, 1973.

```
┌─────────────────┐  ┌─────────────────┐  ┌─────────────┐
│ Food availability│  │ Sleeping/denning│  │  Predation  │
│  & dispersion   │  │site avail.&dispers.│ │  pressure   │
└─────────────────┘  └─────────────────┘  └─────────────┘
```

Group Size ⟷ Population Dispersion

SOCIAL
SYSTEM

Social Structure & Dynamics

FIG. 9. Schema showing the interrelationships between the adaptive patterns of social organization of a given species fitted to a particular set of environmental variables. (After Crook, 1970.)

home range. The young are usually driven from the home territory at nine or ten months of age (when the parents have their subsequent estrus the following spring). The Type 3 social pattern is seen in the wolf; unlike the red fox and the coyote, the wolf does not desert or repel its young, and the young usually stay with the parents. There has been much discussion about the origin of the wolf pack, and the general consensus is that the pack represents an extended family consisting of the mother, her offspring, a male leader (who may or may not be the father), one or two other adults, and one or more subadults from an earlier litter. In some regions the pack splits up during certain times of the year, and there is evidence in Finland and Russia that many packs consist of the mother and her young alone. We know little, however, of such regional variations.

Regional ecological variations over successive generations can lead to racial types differing not only morphologically but also socially and behaviorally. Ecological factors such as abundance, distribution, seasonal availability, and type of major prey may be important determinants (Figure 9). Kümmer (1971) has elegantly shown in baboons that such environmental variables do influence the types of social organization that are manifested by various races or subspecies of this primate. In Canada there is a race of wolves that exists in small packs and specializes in hunting deer. In contrast, there is another type of Canadian wolf, much larger in size, that travels in larger packs and preys on moose. A wolf species (*Canis lupus bailey*) in the mountainous regions of Mexico is rarely seen in packs; these wolves usually travel singly or in pairs. In each of these examples ecological determinants—type, abundance, and distribution of food—influence social behavior.

To what degree are these social patterns genetically determined? There is evidence from people who have hand-raised Mexican wolves that they do tend to be less gregarious than other races of wolves and resemble more the coyote. The Mexican wolf, therefore, is a good example of a Type 3 canid that under ecological selection pressures has become a transitional Type 2 form. Conversely, when there is an abundance of food, Type 2 canids such as the coyote and the golden jackal may exhibit certain social patterns similar to those of the Type 3 canids; the surviving young may stay with the parents for an extra year and may even assist the parents in raising a subsequent generation of offspring. Such observations, however, have never been made in the red fox, a Type 1 canid. It would seem, therefore, that the wolf and the coyote are socioecologically more flexible than the Type 1 fox species. In the latter case we might well postulate that a genetically determined, socioecologically adaptive "innate" program has evolved. We might also ask what keeps wolf and coyote pairs together outside of the two-week-long breeding season. Here we must propose a social need as such, which contrasts sharply with the primarily sexual motivation for the maintenance of pair-bonds in the primate species, including man.

Temperament and Status in Canids

Developmental studies of various canid types have enabled us to identify some of the characteristics of social behavior in the adults and to isolate some of the causes underlying the differences between species. For instance, a litter of red foxes is typically homogeneous in terms of temperament. Most of the cubs are extremely aggressive, assertive, independent, and highly exploratory; at as early as five weeks of age they are able to kill small prey by themselves. In contrast, a litter of wolf cubs does not show the same degree of homogeneity: some individuals are outgoing and aggressive and are very efficient at killing prey while others are so timid that they may become catatonic with fear when presented with live prey and may not investigate novel stimuli placed in the home cage. We find that measures of prey-killing ability and exploratory behavior correlate positively with an individual's social rank at six or eight weeks of age and also in follow-up studies at one and two years of age. It would seem that in the wolf litter the constellation of temperaments represents a nuclear pack structure with one or two leaders, a number of middle-ranking supporters, and a few low-ranking followers (Fox, 1972a).

These findings lead to the hypothesis that in the wolf there has been strong selection in favor of behavioral polymorphism within litters so that under optimal conditions a pack consisting of littermates and one or both parents could form. Pack formation would be impossible if all individuals were of the dominant type or if all individuals were shy subordinates. Indeed, Eskimo hunters report that some wolves in the pack never actually kill prey. They seem to be too timid to kill, but they do back up their companions and, being shy, nervous animals, may well serve as sentinels when the pack is at rest. These early differences in temperament may lead to further social differentiation and role formation later in life. In captive wolf packs we have discovered that a leader and one or two cohorts may work as a triad to exclude or to repress an individual of potentially high rank. In the wild a repressed leader might well emigrate. This has recently been confirmed by Mech (personal communication) in his work with several packs of wolves in Lake Superior National Forest in Minnesota. Through radio collars placed on certain wolves Mech discovered that the individuals that leave the pack are not always aged or inferior subordinate wolves; some of them appear to be young adults who may well be repressed alpha individuals. Such wolves may provide the necessary link between packs to maintain gene flow and to prevent inbreeding within packs that establish exclusive rights to certain home ranges.

In the transitional Type 2 canid such as the coyote we find that the litters are oligomorphic; there are no ranges of temperament as in the wolf, but there is less homogeneity than in the red fox (Fox, 1974). Coyote cubs tend to be either outgoing and self-confident or relatively cautious and timid, yet all are capable of killing prey at an early age.

These early differences in temperament within and between litters of the various canid types are important because they are the foundations for the later development of social behavior in each species. If, for example, a young

FIG. 10. Coyotes and wolves differ markedly in aggressivity. (*top*) Coyote cubs fight at four weeks of age; wolf cubs of the same age are usually very playful. (*bottom*) Resident coyotes threaten a stranger; young wolves investigate the stranger and accept him readily.

red fox were timid, dependent, and incapable of killing prey, it simply would not be able to survive when at four or five months of age it is deserted by its parents and littermates. These findings therefore support the theory that the differences in temperament in the three basic canid types are correlated very closely with the later life style of the species in question whether it is a solitary species (Type 1), a monogamous species with a permanent pair-bond (Type 2), or a communal hunting pack (Type 3).

Studies of aggressive behavior in these canids add another dimension to the overall picture (Fox, 1971a). When young wolves first begin to play at around twenty-one days of age, they do so in a very gentle way, licking and mouthing each other and chewing but not inflicting any injury. Compared to the coyote, they appear to have greater bite control at this age. In sharp contrast, we find that coyotes and red foxes at the same age engage in little play; instead they show a high degree of proximity intolerance accompanied by biting and overt fighting (Figure 10). On more than one occasion we have lost young coyotes between three and four weeks of age as a consequence of these early fights.

Although by five to six weeks of age the bite intensity of coyote and fox cubs is better controlled during play and aggressive interaction, usually no stable kind of dominance hierarchy is formed, whereas in wolf cubs this is evident by six to eight weeks of age. The dominance hierarchy, based upon individual differences in temperament and proximity tolerance, seems to hold the wolf litter together in a pattern in which each individual knows its place. Consequently, once the hierarchy is formed, there is a reduction in conflict and an increase in social control of aggression. Pack formation in wolves is correlated with allelomimetic or group-coordinated behavior coupled with the tendency to follow a leader; in foxes allelomimetic and following behaviors are absent. Possibly the absence of a stable social hierarchy and the highly individualistic temperament of the red fox facilitate fission of the litter. Like the red fox, the coyote appears to show a greater proximity intolerance with increasing age, and in the absence of a firmly established dominance hierarchy this seems to lead ultimately to dispersal of the litter.

In recent studies of physiological differences within wolf litters the heart rates of free-moving subjects were recorded using biotelemeter transmitters; these studies showed that the more dominant and outgoing cubs have a much higher resting heart rate than do their subordinates. This is also true in adult wolves. It would seem, therefore, that the dominant wolves characteristically have a greater sympathetic tone. We have exposed cubs of varying temperament and rank to stress and have found that the plasma cortisol elevation following ACTH injection was minimal in the lowest-ranking cubs while in higher-ranking cubs it followed the norm predicted for optimal response to stress (Fox and Andrews, 1973). Candland and his colleagues (1970) at Bucknell University have found that the heart rate in squirrel monkeys is also correlated with rank. Candland has added further insights into these physiological differences which seem to be primarily based upon some genetic or innate temperament constellation. When he took a squirrel monkey of high rank from one group and placed it in a group where it was low-ranking, its heart rate dropped. Conversely, when he put a middle-ranking squirrel monkey into a group where it became a leader, its resting heart rate increased. We do not know yet to what degree physiological responses in wolves are modifiable as a consequence of social relationships, context, and role, but these factors are certainly relevant to psychosomatic and ecological medicine in humans, where role and context affect physiology as well as responses to stress and disease.

In wolf cubs it seems that a certain set of physiological reactions (which may be genotypic) form the substrate for temperament and thus become the basis for the experiential development of the phenotype. Thomas, Chess, and Birch (1970), working with human neonates, found that they were able to make strong predictions about the subsequent development of a child's personality on the basis of a few physiological and behavioral characteristics which are somewhat comparable to those we have observed in wolf cubs.

Concepts in Ethology

Social Behavior and Communication

Within the wolf pack there is always a leader, usually a male; the leader is rarely female because a female leader that was nursing a litter could not effectively lead the pack. There is accumulating evidence that the leader does not always breed; the male overlord does not have all the females to himself. This would be highly adaptive in that it would prevent an excess of genes from a single individual that maintained his dominance rank for a number of years. Dominance hierarchies also exist among the females (Zimen, 1974). Usually the dominant female mates with the male of her choice. Social relationships are complicated further by certain allegiances between members of the same sex or of opposite sexes and between parents and certain young.

Social relationships in wolf packs change as individuals mature or become aged, and tensions within the pack arise, especially when there is a lack of food or during the breeding season. Combined with a large pack size, these interacting socioecological factors could lead to effective inhibition or disruption of sexual activities and pair formation. The resulting social "birth control" is little understood but seems to operate to ensure that an unusually large number of cubs is only rarely produced.* In most wild packs many of the offspring die in the first winter, and survivors simply fill places made available by the death or occasional emigration of adults.

A frequently observed pack ritual is a collective display of allegiance to the leader. Typically, wolves wake up, stretch, greet each other, and focus much attention on the

---

* Mech (personal communication) finds that when pack density is high the cubs born into the pack include an unusually large proportion of males.

FIG. 11. Group greeting of the pack leader by subordinate wolves. The subordinates wag their tails, whine, and lick the face and bite the muzzle of the leader; the greeting is frequently followed by a group howl.

leader, licking his face, nibbling and jawing his muzzle, wagging their tails, and whining (Figure 11). He might in turn growl and seize various individuals around the muzzle or pin them to the ground and hold them there for a few seconds. This highly ritualized assertion of rank cannot be interpreted as aggressive but rather as a derived activity which now serves to reinforce social bonds. The leader also occasionally performs a ritual which has been observed by both Schenkel (1947) and myself (Fox, 1971a). He will seize some food item or an interesting object such as a bone or a piece of caribou skin and parade with it before the entire pack; then he will approach the pack, drop the object, and leave it. The entire pack briefly investigates the "gift" and then ignores it. This is interpreted by both observers as a ritualized kind of giving which is seen more or less exclusively in the leader wolf.

This leads us to the phenomenon of food-sharing, which, according to most primatologists, is a characteristic only of human primates. In recent personal communications with Stewart Halperin and Jane van Lawick-Goodall, however, I learned that they have observed food-sharing in chimpanzees. Food-sharing is an important aspect of the social life of the wolf, especially while the cubs are being raised. One adult (the mother or an "aunt" or an "uncle") usually remains with the cubs while the rest of the pack goes off hunting. When the members of the pack return, they regurgitate food for the baby-sitter and also for the cubs. Gordon Haber (personal communication), working in Mount McKinley National Park, has seen an adult pack member regularly regurgitate food for a leader who was laid up for several days with an injured foot. Such cases of altruism are not unusual in highly social and interdependent species such as wolves.

When an adult wolf is about to regurgitate food for the cubs, it will often give a few low whines and the cubs come running over. At other times, however, the cubs mob the adult around his mouth until he vomits. This face-oriented mobbing seems to persist into maturity as a derived social greeting. We have found that young adults and subordinates orient toward superiors in the same way, licking the corners and the inside of the superior's mouth (Figure 12). These actions are especially evident during the collective display of allegiance to the leader, which is an example of a number of the derived behaviors discussed in chapter 1. Food-soliciting in cubs therefore becomes greeting and appeasement behavior in adults. Similarly, the submissive side-to-side head movements of a wolf as he approaches a

FIG. 12. Ritualized aggression. (*top*) The dominant wolf seizes the muzzle of the subordinate. (*bottom*) The subordinate subsequently licks the superior's mouth in a derived infantile display of appeasement.

superior and the upward rooting movements when he makes contact are action patterns identical to those of a cub in locating the teat and initiating nursing. Schenkel agrees that these actions in the adult are derived from neonatal nursing patterns.

Concepts in Ethology

One of the most intriguing and best documented examples of a derived activity is the inguinal response (Fox, 1971a) which is seen in the coyote, the wolf, and to a lesser extent in the domesticated dog (Figure 5). When a socialized adult is touched in the groin or the inguinal region, it remains passive. When two adult dogs or wolves make social contact with each other, one invariably orients toward the groin of the other. Groin presentation is usually manifested by the subordinate individual. As a social gesture, it is perhaps analogous to a handshake in man. The next time you see a friendly dog approaching you, notice how he wiggles his head and swings one hip around, presenting the groin. If you touch him in the groin, he will remain completely passive and may even roll over onto one side in complete submission. He may then urinate submissively. Submissive urination is the final clue to the ontogenetic history of this behavior. When wolves, coyotes, and dogs are very young, they are unable to urinate, and the mother reflexively stimulates urination by licking the genitalia. During stimulation the pups remain passive while the mother nuzzles the groin region. Later, of course, the animals are able to control urination voluntarily, but the behavior trait of remaining passive when the groin is touched persists as part of their social repertoire. The inhibition of urination in the pups until the mother stimulates them is highly adaptive in the wild because if the cubs were constantly urinating and defecating while the mother was away, the den would be uninhabitable in a few days. As it is, during the first three or four weeks they only eliminate when the mother stimulates them and ingests their excrement.

All the complex and subtly integrated displays of the wolf (Figure 13) serve to increase, decrease, or maintain a

FIG. 13. Schema of gross body displays of the wolf in different motivational contexts. *1.* Threat or dominance display. *2, 3.* Ambivalent; defensive threat with increasing fear. *4.* Fear; passive submission. *5.* Lateral recumbent position in passive submissive display. *6.* Paw-raising and bow of active submissive greeting. *7.* Play-soliciting posture.

certain social distance between conspecifics (Fox, 1971a). Other signals arouse or orient individuals. Wolves effectively regulate social distance through eye contact; as in man, avoidance of eye contact is a signal of submission while a direct stare is a threat. A dominant wolf can put down another from fifty yards or more with a direct stare. Even at this distance the subordinate looks away and may whine and lower its tail and ears. If the subordinate approaches, the superior may turn away and break eye contact; this has been interpreted by Schenkel as daring the subordinate to attack, but I have not seen subordinates show the slightest aggression at these times. When the dominant wolf looks away from the subordinate wolf, it is the equivalent of a person giving a "cold shoulder" to another by looking away in response to a greeting.

Konrad Lorenz has said in several books that the submissive wolf or dog presents its throat to a superior as a sign of complete submission. This may be a misinterpretation of what is actually going on. The subordinate is, in fact, avoiding eye contact, often in a very exaggerated fashion which frequently includes the elevation of one forepaw and a readiness to roll over onto one side in complete submission. The animal is not presenting its throat. If the subordinate were attacked, the rules of the anatomy of aggression would be followed, and the cheek, the muzzle, or the shoulder region would be bitten. Wolves and dogs go for each other's throats only when it is an extreme rivalry fight (to the death), and at such times looking away is not seen.

A bright-eyed direct look is often given during friendly approach, especially during play, and it is in this eye contact pattern, combined with what is termed the play face, that we again find certain analogies with human communication. During friendly approach, especially with the intention to play, canids open the mouth slightly and pull the lips back horizontally. They often pant, and the red fox vocalizes slightly at this time. Van Hooff (1967) has described the same facial expression in chimpanzees, terming it the panting play face. At the same time the chimpanzee may vocalize a sound very much like laughter in man. We can say, therefore, that canids do have an ancestral, primitive antecedent of laughter as we know it in *Homo sapiens*. Canids also have a submissive grin (Figure 14) which is analogous to the obsequious, no-tooth smile the office boy gives to the boss.

FIG. 14. Schema of facial expressions in the coyote, illustrating simultaneous and successive combinations. *1-3*. Erect ears, small mouth, and aggressive pucker (anterohorizontal contraction of the lips) give way to an open-mouth threat with vertical retraction of the lips. *4-9*. Ear postures shift, and the neck is held more horizontally; the submissive "grin" (posterohorizontal contraction of the lips) combines with varying degrees of open-mouth threat and vertical retraction of the lips. (From Fox, 1971a.)

The threat or aggressive face of the canid entails a pushing forward of the lips to make a small mouth. This is the first grade of aggressive intensity in the wolf. In the second grade of intensity a vertical retraction of the lips is added to display the canine teeth. In primates including man the pushing forward and puckering of the mouth during threat are very similar to threat expressions in the canids. The lips are pushed forward and then, with increasing intensity or arousal, are vertically retracted (Figure 15).

FIG. 15. The range of facial expressions in the fox and the wolf. Facial expressions in the fox: *a*, *h*, the open-mouth threat stare; *b*, the threat stare; *c*, *f*, the greeting "grin"; *d*, *e*, the open-mouth play face; *g*, the defensive gape. Note that the fox cannot retract the lips vertically to form a snarl. (*facing page*) Facial expressions in the wolf: *a*, the alert "smile"; *b*, *g*, the threat stare; *c*, *f*, the offensive threat stare; *d*, *k*, *m*, various submissive expressions; *e*, the defensive threat stare; *h*, the greeting "grin"; *i*, *j*, the open-mouth play face; *l*, the consummatory face (with the eyes closed) while eating.

Animal and Human Hunting Groups

Several primatologists and anthropologists have suggested that observations of the wolf pack might produce a number of insights relevant to our understanding of primitive human hunting groups which the study of nonhuman primates that do not hunt cannot provide. Evidence gleaned from archaeological records and also from the few hunting and gathering societies that remain (the !Kung Bushmen, the

Australian aborigines, and certain South American hunters) gives us some knowledge of our ancestral past. The excellent book *Man the Hunter*, edited by Lee and DeVore, contains several reviews that discuss such things as home range, optimal size of the group, aspects of territoriality, and leadership in primitive hunting and gathering societies. These studies show how man and wolf, in adapting to similar sets of ecological conditions, have independently evolved comparable social (and possibly genetic) means of coping with their environment.

It should be remembered that 90 percent of our existence as *Homo sapiens* was spent as hunters and gatherers, so that although many of our contemporary social needs may seem anachronistic if not actually maladaptive, they are derived from thousands of years of cultural and socioecological selection. For instance, we like to be in small groups. Furthermore, males like to be with males, as Lionel Tiger has shown in his book *Men in Groups*; in Tiger's view this preference in contemporary man is based upon a primitive or ancestral need for males to be together in all-male hunting parties and ritual ceremonies. The evolution of cooperative hunting with weapons seems to be the link between the nonhuman primate and man, and this new activity generated new social needs and a more complex brain. Just as the wolf pack developed built-in rituals to control aggression and to reduce mortal injuries from the use of the canine teeth, so with the emergence of weapons primitive man adopted various rituals and laws to reduce internecine strife.

In all hunting societies there seems to be a close correlation between the size of the group and the availability of food. Wolf packs frequently contain about ten individuals and utilize an area of 500 to 1,000 square miles, and a human hunting and gathering society might consist of thirty individuals using a home range of some 1,000 to 1,500 square miles. Compare these figures with similar figures for other primate species: a troop of forty baboons might utilize a home range of some 15 square miles, and a band of fifteen or so gorillas might require a home range of no more than 30 or 40 square miles. The fact that cooperative hunting requires the exploitation of a much larger home range may be related to the fact that man, like the wolf, became a great wanderer. It might also be tied in with modern man's wanderlust and his need for varied environmental stimulation.

The successful exploitation of a large home range entails the ability to remember features of the terrain, what

The Behavior of Wolves, Dogs, and Man

food plants are available and when and where, where prey can be found and most advantageously ambushed, and so on. The survival of both the wolf pack and the human hunting and gathering group depends on their ability to obtain and utilize this information and to hand it down from one generation to the next. Other vital information such as the location of water holes and denning sites also has to be transmitted generationally. Finally, it is possible to draw more tenuous analogies between the group rituals of animals and man. The "love-ins" or allegiance displays in greeting the leader wolf (often followed by the pack's howling together) and gift-giving by the leader wolf have counterparts in dance ceremonies, gift-giving, and displays to the leader and the elders in hunting and gathering societies.

Domestication and Civilization

We will now consider some of the effects of domestication in the dog which are revealed by a comparison of certain behavior patterns in dogs and wolves. This will enable us to draw analogies between the behavioral consequences of domestication in the dog and the effects of cultural evolution or civilization in man.

Wolves do not reach sexual maturity until the second year of life, and they breed only once a year in the winter, ensuring that the offspring are born in the spring when there will be an abundance of prey. In contrast, domestic dogs, through selective breeding, are sexually precocious; the first heat may occur at the age of six months, and all breeds have two and occasionally three heats per year. In addition, while male wolves produce sperm only during the breeding season, male dogs are constantly potent.

Concepts in Ethology

There is good evidence that wolves and especially coyotes (although the coyote is probably not one of the progenitors of the dog) are monogamous; at least they show very strong mate preferences. In domesticated dogs, however, any inclination toward monogamy or strong mate preferences has been virtually eliminated in the course of selective breeding. Nevertheless, recent work by Beach and LeBoeuf (1967) has shown that female beagles, if given the opportunity, will choose one particular male over another, although the basis for such discrimination has not been identified.

I have found that as wolves get older they become increasingly wary of strangers; my male wolf, for instance, shows marked aggression toward certain men but, interestingly enough, not usually toward women. In the wild this increasing wariness and avoidance of strangers could well serve to keep the pack together and to limit its size; strange wolves are either avoided or are actively driven away. But like my hand-raised wolves, wolves in the wild maintain their affection for those with whom they were raised (parents, aunts, and uncles). In domestic dogs, except perhaps in guard dogs, this trait has been modified so that social attachments become generalized to include all or most human beings (Fox, 1971a). Somewhere along the line, therefore, the innate sociability of the dog has been changed considerably in adapting to domesticated life with man. Possibly the readiness of the dog to accept strangers is related to its greater dependency on man. The tendency of the wolf to avoid strangers is perhaps analogous to xenophobia in man. Ethologists regard such phenomena as ethological barriers; by preventing gene flow between groups which are genetically adapted to certain niches, these barriers enhance the possibilities of local adaptation to given sets of ecological conditions.

The Behavior of Wolves, Dogs, and Man

It is occasionally noted that a dog will become shy at about five months of age for no apparent reason. Although he is friendly toward people, he becomes distrustful of unusual objects or things he has never seen before; some dogs do not outgrow this. The syndrome is a typical trait of the wild canid and can be observed in wolves, coyotes, and jackals and in wolf-dog and coyote-dog hybrids. It would seem that the domestic dogs that show this trait are regressing to a wild or ancestral pattern, and the low incidence of the trait would suggest that early in the course of domestication this behavior was selectively bred out of most dogs. In the wild, on the other hand, it would be highly adaptive for a young animal to react very cautiously toward any change in its familiar terrain because such a change could mean danger.

Richter (1954), in his comparisons of the behavior of wild and laboratory rats, proposes that in domestication there has been a strong selection for gonadal hyperactivity and adrenal hypoactivity. Beylaev and Trut (1974) have added more information on this topic by selectively breeding silver foxes for docility. After fifteen generations of inbreeding, during which the foxes have become increasingly more docile, Beylaev and Trut find that some of the foxes have a tendency to develop two heats instead of one per year and that they do not react inappropriately or maladaptively to stress. Their stress responses are very similar to those that we have observed in our dominant wolf cubs. It should be added that the dominant wolf cubs tend to be more sociable than their subordinates toward human beings, even though none of the cubs has been hand-raised and all have had similar exposure to people. Perhaps, therefore, the process of domestication involves a modification of both the pituitary-gonadal and pituitary-adrenal relationships as pro-

Concepts in Ethology

posed by Richter and partially confirmed by Beylaev and Trut.

The increased reproductive capacities of domestic dogs may be correlated with the increased reproductive potential and high sexual activity of *Homo sapiens*. We find that the fertility of most primates which live in an area where there is a seasonal decline in the availability of food is restrained to a short period during the year. In this way pregnancy and the birth of young in these primates (as in canids) are synchronized with a relative abundance of food. Those primates living in a more equable environment such as a lush jungle where there is a constant abundance of food, on the other hand, tend to have a cyclic estrus like the cyclic menstrual patterns of the human female, and the males tend to be always potent like the human male, although the nonhuman female primates are only receptive to the males during part of their cycle. It is possible that the constant sexual receptivity of the human female has developed as a means of maintaining the strong pair-bond and family structure essential to the survival of human offspring, which require an extended period of parental care.

A common problem in domestic dogs is the development of increasing aggressiveness at about one or two years of age (Fox, 1972b). Quite suddenly a dog may begin to test its owner and may seem to be attempting to elevate itself to the dominant alpha position in the human "pack." At this time the dog often shows increasing aggression toward intruders onto its territory. This behavior occurs in the wolf at about the same age and is related to sexual maturity; in the dog it is dissociated from sexual maturity because in the process of domestication the dog has become sexually potent much earlier in life. In domestic dogs castration has a significant effect in lowering territorial

The Behavior of Wolves, Dogs, and Man

aggression and in reducing rivalry with household companions.

It is possible to draw an analogy between the many specialized breeds of dogs and the many roles of modern man. The various dog breeds—pointers, bloodhounds, guard dogs, and so on—are superb examples of genetic engineering (selective breeding), and their specialized functions are analogous to specialized roles in man. In dogs the more specialized the individual becomes, the less flexible or utilitarian he is. Specialization in dogs is genotypic because certain behaviors are at a lower threshold than in man and are more accessible to reinforcement and training. But it is possible that some kinds of specialization have also occurred in man—visual and olfactory acuity are far greater in Bushmen than in Europeans, for example.

Intelligence and trainability are often correlated in the dog. Wolves, however, are very difficult to train even when they have been hand-raised. The basis for trainability is partly linked with early socialization (Scott and Fuller, 1965). It has been shown by Scott and Fuller that if socialization is delayed (that is, if puppies are not taken as pets before they are about twelve weeks of age) they are difficult to train. Trainability in the dog is also enhanced by dependency. One way of making a dog dependent is to socialize it so that it becomes emotionally attached to its master early in life; another way is through genetic selection. We now have evidence from our laboratory studies that adult domestic dogs exhibit more infantile behavior (neoteny) and dependency toward people than do wild canids raised under the same conditions. Many writers have emphasized that in man, too, neoteny has played an important role in evolution. In fact, some go so far as to say that without our neotenous potential (which allows us to prolong maturation to facilitate the acquisition of

Concepts in Ethology

information from culture and which gives us the capacity to modify early acquired behaviors) man would not have any capacity for culture at all. (Dobzhansky, for one, proposes that educability in man is inherited.) Therefore, extending the analogy somewhat further, we find that neoteny plays a very important role in both the domestication of animals and in the development of civilization in man.

One final point is warranted in connection with territoriality. As crowding increases among dogs, home valency or the value of territory also increases and the animal is motivated more and more to defend its territory through aggressive displays, barking, urinating, and even attacking. Certainly in many urban and suburban areas where large dog populations may result in crowding there is a hypertrophy of territorial behavior. A parallel to this may exist in human behavior. Sociologists and psychiatrists have proposed that a man's home and his plot of land become increasingly important if he feels a loss of identity or a lack of fulfillment in crowded urban life. A pathological kind of hypertrophy of his sense of home base or of territory may develop, coupled with paranoid insecurity that the territory might be violated and robbed.

More concrete analogies between human and animal behavior and experimental models of behavioral and developmental abnormalities in animals which throw light on the etiology of similar disorders in man will be described in the next section.

CHAPTER 3

NORMAL AND ABNORMAL BEHAVIOR DEVELOPMENT

Phenomenologically similar ontogenetic processes evident in a wide range of species provide the basis for making certain theoretical generalizations, some of which are of applied (clinical) value. In terms of etiology and clinical signs many disorders in humans and animals are similar and provide a basis for comparative psychopathology. Much of the animal data that will be reviewed in this section is from controlled experiments on laboratory animals; these data constitute an invaluable body of reference material for clinical cases in both veterinary and human medicine. The approaches of ethologists and psychiatrists to the analysis of adaptive and maladaptive behaviors, respectively, have traditionally involved both developmental (etiological) and phenomenological perspectives. In this review some of the findings from ethology and developmental psychobiology will be presented in order to demonstrate the importance of

NOTE: This chapter is based on a lecture in the Wesley W. Spink Lectures on Comparative Medicine presented at the University of Minnesota, Duluth campus, on October 17, 1973.

Concepts in Ethology

findings that offer a phylogenetic as well as an ontogenetic perspective to psychopathology. Psychiatrists are becoming increasingly aware of the limitations of studying the human species per se and are finding that they can learn more about the etiology of certain human disorders when the developmental and phylogenetic perspectives of comparative psychopathology are utilized.

Imprinting and Socialization

The concept of a "critical period" implies that experience at a particular time of development is essential for normal development to continue (Fox, 1971b). This is exemplified by the phenomenon of imprinting in birds. Imprinting means attachment, and birds (such as ducklings) which are relatively mature when hatched normally become imprinted onto the mother during the first few hours after hatching. If they are taken as soon as they are hatched and are raised not with the mother but with a human being, a flashing red light, or a moving cardboard box, they become preferentially attached to the species or the object with which they have been raised. Some reversal is possible during subsequent weeks, but there is strong evidence that this early exposure results in a very specific and enduring attachment—so enduring that at maturity social and sexual behavior may be directed toward the same stimulus to which the bird was imprinted early in life.

Lorenz (1970) hand-raised jackdaws and crows and found that when they reached maturity they would show courtship behavior toward him and would attempt to mount his hand; during the time when they would normally be taking care of their own young, they would attempt to stuff grubs into his ears. Hediger (1950) describes the experience of one of his zoo keepers who hand-raised a male moose.

Normal and Abnormal Behavior Development

When the moose reached sexual maturity, the keeper led it into a field of female moose and the young bull became sexually aroused. Instead of directing his sexual behavior toward a female moose, however, he attempted to mount his keeper. Such bizarre behaviors are good examples of the enduring effect of imprinting in determining later social and sexual preferences in various animals. Klinghammer (1967) has shown that the effects of hand-rearing in various species of pigeons can vary. One species, for example, if hand-raised, shows a sexual preference at maturity directed exclusively toward its human handler rather than toward its own species while closely related species show a reversal at maturity; although still friendly toward the human foster parent, they are only sexually attracted to their own species. Klinghammer also identifies a third category of pigeons in which individuals have the best of both worlds and show sexual behavior toward both their own species and the foster parent!

It is also known that the two sexes of a given species are not affected in the same way by imprinting. In mallards, for example, Schutz (1965) finds that early imprinting in the males later determines their sexual preference while female mallards, regardless of imprinting, show an innate preference for males of their own species. This was confirmed by raising male and female mallards with different species of ducks. When they reached maturity, the male mallards preferred the species with which they had been cross-fostered while the female mallards tended to reverse their social preferences in sexual encounters and to seek out males of their own species.

We have raised dogs with cats during the critical period of socialization to evaluate further the effects of cross-fostering. In this study a three-week-old chihuahua was placed with a litter of four-week-old kittens. Five replications of the study were done (Fox, 1971b), and in each replication a battery of tests was given to the pup at twelve weeks of age. It was found that the pups raised with kittens made no social responses to their own mirror images; they literally lacked species recognition. They also preferred the company of cats to that of the littermate chihuahuas which were used as controls. The cats that had been raised with a dog were also sociable toward dogs that had not been raised with cats. In contrast, cats that had had no earlier exposure to dogs avoided contact with them—with one exception. Salzen and Cornell (1968) did a comparable study for color preferences in chicks which reminds us of the role integrated schools might play in achieving interracial socialization. They raised a green-dyed chicken with a group of red-dyed chickens. When they placed these chickens together with a new group of chickens that were all dyed green, the green chicken ran toward his red companions and did not mix with the green group. Variations on this experiment seem to confirm that allegiances and social preferences are based on early social learning.

Even more subtle consequences of early rearing can affect social preferences. In one experiment we used three groups of pups: the pups in one group were hand-raised and were exposed only to humans; the pups in the second group were weaned early and had almost equal contact with humans and dogs up to the point of testing; the pups in the third group were raised with each other (Fox, 1971b). When the pups were placed in new social groups, it was found that they tended to segregate themselves in accordance with their rearing history. The pups that had been hand-raised and had no social experience with their own

FIG. 16. Approach scores of differentially reared dogs. The approach to a human being of pups II and CI, which had contact with humans early in life, is consistently faster than that of pups which had little contact with humans until weaning at eight weeks. This demonstrates how the reinforcing qualities of human contact (reward) are influenced by early socialization. (From Fox, 1971b.)

kind tended to stay together while the pups that were weaned early and the controls tended to segregate into like groups. Other aspects of social behavior were also affected (Figures 16 and 17).

Sackett, Porter, and Holmes (1965) found a very similar social consequence of early rearing experiences in young rhesus monkeys. They too used three groups: one group was hand-raised exclusively with people; the second group had contact only with other monkeys; the third group had more or less equal contact with humans and their own kind. The monkeys segregated into like groups for social play during early life and later clearly demonstrated sexual preferences based upon their rearing experience. This prompts an anthropomorphic speculation that individuals in human dyads may be compatible because they have grown up within similar subcultures and have similar socioeconomic back-

	A. INTERACTION PREFERENCE	
	HUMAN	DOG
II	122.0 sec. (70-155)	19.0 sec. (0-45)
CI	99.5 sec. (57-129)	25.5 sec. (0-45)
CCI	97.0 sec. (57-159)	40.0 sec. (0-82)

	B. DISTRESS VOCALIZATION SCORE	
	HUMAN	DOG
II	10	2
CI	10	2
CCI	10	8

FIG. 17. Social preference scores for differentially reared dogs. In a choice situation at twelve weeks of age hand-raised pups (II) preferred contact with a human to contact with a passive adult dog. Littermates weaned at three and a half weeks and then dog-deprived (CI) and others weaned at eight weeks and dog-deprived (CCI) showed more interest in the dog. Similarly, when the pups were placed behind a barrier, all pups vocalized distress to a person, but only the CCI pups vocalized significantly to an adult dog. (From Fox, 1971b.)

grounds with comparable patterns of child-rearing and socialization.

If social experiences are denied during the early critical period, as demonstrated in our cat-dog socialization study, there is often impairment in the subsequent development of social relationships. Scott and Fuller (1965), working in Bar Harbor, showed that if dogs are denied human contact until approximately fourteen weeks of age they are wild and unapproachable. Scott and Fuller demonstrated clearly the critical nature of the socialization process and found that human contact between six and eight weeks of age seems to be optimal for the socialization of dogs.

Although there is an optimal period for socializing pups, there is evidence that dogs may subsequently regress or become feral. The social bond with man may be broken when well-socialized pups are placed in kennels at three or

Normal and Abnormal Behavior Development

four months of age; by six or eight months they are shy of strangers and often of their caretakers if they have not been handled much. In addition, they may be extremely fearful when removed from their usual quarters. Their fearfulness is the result of a combination of institutionalization and desocialization. In connection with the phenomenon of desocialization Woolpy (1968) found that captive wild adult wolves can be socialized in six months of careful handling and that when they are subsequently given less human contact they do not regress or become desocialized. In contrast, wolves that are socialized early in life are like dogs in that they will regress if they are subsequently given less human contact. These findings suggest therefore that although there is an optimal period early in life when socialization can be rapidly established, subsequent reinforcement is necessary because of some intrinsic instability of retention in young animals. Woolpy (1968) concluded that "an important aspect of socialization is learning to cope with a previously unfamiliar environmental situation in the presence of unreduced subjective fear. . . . We have interpreted the results of both the tranquilizer and the socialization experiments to indicate that the fear of the unfamiliar is the primary obstacle to wolf socialization and that, while the overt responses of fear appear very early in life, its subjective components continue to develop throughout at least the first year. Socialization must be conditioned in the presence of the fully developed subjective components of fear, and hence it cannot be permanently maintained in juveniles if they are left to develop fear responses subsequent to having become socialized in early life."

There seems to be a comparable critical period for the development of emotional attachments in children. Bowlby (1971), from the Tavistock Clinic in London, has placed much emphasis upon the critical nature of infant socialization in determining later socially adjustive behavior and in preventing delinquency and even antisocial and sociopathic behaviors. He has demonstrated that traumatic separation of the infant from the mother during the critical attachment period can have long-lasting effects on the child's later emotionality and social behavior. Just as we know that it is best to take a puppy as a pet when it is between six and eight weeks of age, it is now recognized that there is an optimal time for adopting a human infant, preferably before the infant is three months old (before the onset of the critical period for socialization). An orphan who has spent his or her early months in an institution and has developed no close attachment to any particular caretaker may never develop a close relationship to anyone later in life. It seems that in both animals and humans the initial or primary socialization early in life is the basis for the development of subsequent secondary social relationships, and if primary attachments are not made or are in some way modified the consequences for the later social adjustment of the individual can be quite serious.

Early Experiences and Development

Schneirla (1965) has developed a very important theory involving the significance of approach-withdrawal processes in the organization and development of behavior. For instance, approach and subsequent reward (such as contact comfort) are tied in with parasympathetic arousal while withdrawal from painful stimulation is associated with adrenal-sympathetic arousal. If contact comfort, especially that associated with nursing, causes parasympathetic arousal (exemplified in the human infant by salivation, increased peristalsis, secretion of digestive juices, general relaxation,

Normal and Abnormal Behavior Development

and occasionally penile erection), then we have good evidence not of a hedonistic model as proposed in Freud's concept of oral gratification but rather of a physiological foundation for the effects of petting and mothering per se. Young animals derive considerable reward from contact comfort, grooming, and nursing; if the same circumstances cause parasympathetic arousal, then contact comfort, grooming, and nursing would tend to improve digestion and assimilation of food as well as to facilitate emotional attachment.

Several years ago Spitz (1949) demonstrated that inadequate mothering, which may be reinterpreted as inadequate parasympathetic arousal, led to a wasting disease in many orphan children. They did not gain weight, they did not adequately digest and assimilate their food, and many succumbed to infections. When Spitz initiated a regime of mothering, the infants began to gain weight, and the rate of mortality decreased significantly. This effect, distinct from the handling effect, has been termed gentling. We need much more research into the psychological and physiological processes underlying this phenomenon. It might throw new light on Harlow's (1965) observations that infant rhesus monkeys prefer a warm, soft, terry-cloth mother to a wire one and a rocking, moving mother to static one, and it might also give us a new way of looking at Freud's theories about erotogenic areas and of interpreting physiologically his concepts of oral gratification and frustration. Frustration might be indicative of inadequate parasympathetic arousal or, conversely, excessive sympathetic arousal which could be unnecessarily stressful to the infant during a sensitive period early in life.

The psychoanalytic theory of personality development based on the oral, anal, and genital developmental stages of

Freud incorporates the idea that during particular periods early in life certain modalities or areas of sensory perception attain sufficient maturity so that experiences via these channels influence subsequent development. For instance, each person has a certain amount of psychic energy or libido; if an individual's libido becomes fixated at an early stage or regresses during psychosexual development, the adult libido remains attached to activities appropriate to the early stage of development. We may postulate that parasympathetic and sympathetic arousing stimuli form the basis for the developing personality, since the dichotomous autonomic nervous system is the first channel through which external stimuli may influence (possibly even prenatally) the developing child. Thus with early "object" (parental) loss or improper mothering the autonomic nervous system may be affected; the parasympathetic "pleasure" component may not be gratified and the sympathetic component may not be sufficiently de-aroused through nursing and contact comfort. Subsequent emotional frustrations added to these early autonomic imbalances may have severe social and emotional ramifications. For example, the fact that the alcoholic regresses to oral gratification to ease anxiety may be rooted in some perinatal autonomic-experiential trauma.

Although we cannot attempt to present here a full review of the psychoanalytic theory of development, we must emphasize the role of the autonomic nervous system and its "tuning" in relation to arousal and motivation in the neonate. Contactual comfort and oral gratification (sucking, ingestion, and the reduction of hunger and sucking drives) are the first sensory experiences to which the neonate is exposed. The brief description earlier of Schneirla's theory hardly does it justice, but it shows clearly how his psychobiological concepts accord with psychoanalytic theory.

FIG. 18. Stimulus input in infant rats related to emotionality in adulthood. High stimulus input (handling) in infancy is correlated with low emotional reactivity in adulthood. The reverse is true with minimal stimulation or "isolation swaddling" in a stress-minimizing laboratory environment. (From Denenberg, 1964.)

There is a dire need for more rigorous physiological analysis of the gradual emergence of areas of experience (or of modality-related receptor-effector systems) during development.

A number of independent studies on rodents support Schneirla's theory, demonstrating that experimental manipulations early in life can have long-lasting effects on later behavior. For instance, if a five-day-old rat is taken out of its nest and is placed in a metal pot at room temperature for three minutes a day for five days and then is allowed to mature, as an adult it is less emotional than littermates not treated in this way. It may also be more resistant to physical stress such as terminal starvation, cold exposure, and certain pathogens. This effect, which has been called the early handling effect, seems to influence the adrenal-pituitary axis of the developing rodent. Denenberg (1967), Levine and Mullins (1966), and other workers have studied this phenomenon in great detail. It would appear that the stress to which the neonate is exposed in some way affects the way in which it responds to psychological and physical stresses later in life (Figure 18). It has been proposed that a hormonostat exists in the neurohypophysis which is "tuned" to the adrenal glands during the sensitive period when the rat is between five and ten days of age. When this is tuned experimentally by a sudden elevation of corticosteroids during the sensitive period, the hormonostat operates differently when the organism is stressed in maturity. Typically, as Levine has demonstrated, the stress response in adult control rats is somewhat maladaptive. There is a long latency period before the neuroendocrine system responds, but the eventual response can be long-lasting and at times may trigger the onset of Selye's stress syndrome. Early-handled rats have a much shorter latency of response and the duration of response is shorter. In effect, their reactions are not unduly delayed and they do not over-react.

In some strains of mice that develop spontaneous leukemia the onset of the condition can be delayed by this handling procedure. Handled mice also have a greater resistance than non-handled controls to implanted tumors. There are also genetic or strain differences, as demonstrated by Ginsburg (1968). For one strain a given level of stimulation might be excessive; in another strain the sensitive period might lie between postnatal days 6 and 10 or between postnatal days 10 and 15. Ginsburg emphasizes that in a typically heterogeneous population, as in *Homo sapiens*, there would be a normal distribution curve and that individuals would have different sensitive periods as

FIG. 19. Comparison of heart rates of handled dogs and controls. Early handling of pups not only accelerates EEG development but can also affect the autonomic nervous system. Increased sympathetic tone is reflected here in the sustained tachycardia observed in dogs over three weeks of age. (From Fox, 1971b.)

well as different response thresholds. In view of these individual and genetic variations, therefore, we must be very careful in making generalizations about the handling effect.

Levine points out that in the relatively overswaddled laboratory environment neonate rats may well be understressed and that the handling procedure is much closer to the kind of experience they would normally have in the wild. Under natural conditions the mother frequently leaves the nest to forage for food and there are various environmental changes, all of which could have an additive effect resulting in an adult animal that is psychophysiologically superior to the overswaddled laboratory specimen.

In a study of the handling phenomenon in dogs (Fox, 1971b) pups were subjected to varied stimulation—exposure to cold, vestibular stimulation on a tilting board, exposure to flashing lights, and auditory stimulation—from birth until five weeks of age. The pups in the study differed from the controls in a number of ways including earlier maturation of EEG, lowered emotionality which enhanced problem-solving ability in novel situations, and dominance over controls in competitive situations. Analysis of their adrenal glands indicated a fivefold increase in norepinephrine, and studies of their heart rates indicated that a greater sympathetic tone was developed as a consequence of the early handling stress (Figure 19). Meier (1961) demonstrated comparable maturation of EEG and behavioral changes in super-stimulated Siamese kittens. Arshevskii has been applying the concept of early stimulation in human neonates and reports marked differences in the rates of maturation of locomotor ability, verbal ability, and learning ability.

We cannot make a generalization about optimal handling for a given species. For instance, it appears possible that a given level of early stimulation may produce psychophysiological superiority in some human infants and pathophysiological inferiority in certain other individuals. As Thomas, Chess, and Birch (1970) have demonstrated in their longitudinal studies of human infants, handling has to be very carefully adjusted to the basic temperament and autonomic tuning of the individual. The effects of early handling appear to be on the adrenal-sympathetic system, and the research evidence suggests that early handling not only resets the pituitary-adrenal axis but in some way influences autonomic tuning and temperament or emotionality.

Many of the old books for midwives and expectant mothers advise that the pregnant woman should always keep a smile on her face because her frown might be cast on her fetus and remain with it forever. Recent developmental studies tend to confirm some aspects of this old notion. It

Normal and Abnormal Behavior Development

has been shown that prenatal anxiety can have a significant effect on the emotionality and the later personality development of an infant (Joffe, 1969). Thompson (1957) was one of the first to demonstrate the effects of prenatal anxiety on the behavior of offspring. He developed a conditioned emotional reaction in rats placed in a shuttle box; whenever a bell rang, the rats had to jump to the "safe" side of the box in order to avoid shock. The basis for an emotional reaction was established by placing a barrier in the center of the box so that the animals could not jump to the safe side when the bell rang. Since the rats were never given shock when the bell rang after the barrier was erected, the reaction, therefore, was purely emotional. The offspring of pregnant rats that were stressed in this way were cross-fostered by normal mothers in order to control for any postnatal transfer effects from the mother. Thompson found that the prenatally stressed rats were much more emotional than the controls and that their learning abilities were inferior because heightened emotionality interfered with their performance. He was able to produce a similar effect by injecting adrenalin and ACTH into pregnant females.

Joffe (1969) has reviewed many such experiments including his own on the Maudsley reactive and nonreactive strains of rats. He was able to demonstrate genetic differences in susceptibility to prenatal stress as well as differences correlated with the sex of the offspring and the period during pregnancy when the stress was administered. He discovered that premating stress could also have a significant effect on the behavior and the reactivity of the offspring. These experiments emphasize that the developing phenotype is modifiable not only after birth but also prenatally, the effect being mediated by the neuroendocrine system.

Concepts in Ethology

When pregnant rats are gently handled during gestation, it has been found that their offspring are less emotional and easier to handle. No hormone has yet been identified, but it is possible that the gentling of pregnant rats influences the parasympathetic nervous system and that certain neurohumors affect the developing fetus. In this context we should consider the teratogenic effect on humans (for instance, phocomelia) of various drugs and also the possibility that prenatal anxiety states could have harmful effects on the behavior of offspring. At the same time we should investigate the potential benefits which might result from an optimally non-anxiety-provoking environment during pregnancy. More than one proponent of Yoga has stressed the importance of meditation and relaxation for pregnant women in the belief that these activities have a beneficial effect on fetal development and on the later behavior of the offspring. The physiological changes associated with meditation—relaxation and parasympathetic arousal with the slowing of many bodily functions including heart rate, respiration, and metabolism—might well be analogous to the effects of gentling in rats.

These prenatal and postnatal studies in modifying the phenotype also serve to remind us that we know relatively little about how to provide environmental stimulation and rearing programs which will ensure that the developing phenotype can be optimized or at least how it can be protected from deleterious influences. There is much discussion about genetic engineering and programmed breeding through artificial insemination, but we have barely begun to explore the effects of environmental phenomena that are present during certain critical and sensitive periods in development. To cite just one instance, for many years premature babies typically have been swaddled in incubators

Normal and Abnormal Behavior Development

and have been handled very little because of the fear of infections and other deleterious effects, yet recent evidence shows that premature babies do much better when they receive a good deal of handling or when they are placed in a small sling and are given rhythmic rocking stimulation.

Environmental Enrichment and Deprivation

In *The Descent of Man* Darwin observed that the domesticated rabbit has a much smaller brain than its wild counterpart and attributed this to the cumulative effect of generations of captivity during which each generation received far less stimulation than it would in the wild. To test the effect of environmental stimulation on captive animals, Bennett and his coworkers (1964) at the Lawrence Radiation Laboratory in California raised rats in enriched environments. Typical laboratory rats were placed in a large cage with companions and with various objects (wheels, runways, and so on) to manipulate. Under these conditions of environmental complexity Bennett found that the rats in the study became more exploratory than the controls and that they developed significant differences in brain size, in the depth of the visual cortex, and also in the turnover rates of brain acetylcholinesterase. More recently Bennett has demonstrated that the enrichment effect is dependent upon an interaction between the inanimate environment and conspecifics. That is, if a rat is raised alone in an enriched environment, profound changes in brain and behavior do not occur; nor do they occur if a rat is raised with companions in a barren cage.

We have raised dogs under a schedule of paced increments of experience, periodically taking some of them out of their home cages and letting them explore an arena containing novel stimuli (Fox, 1971b). Those that were allowed in the arena at five, eight, twelve, and sixteen weeks of age for a mere half hour per exposure explored increasingly as they grew older and developed a preference for more complex stimuli as they matured. Littermates that were placed in the arena for the first time at twelve or sixteen weeks of age did not explore; they withdrew or did not leave the start chamber, and many of them were catatonic with fear. We are dealing here with an institutionalization syndrome: those dogs that did not have an opportunity to leave their home cages until sometime after eight weeks of age could not tolerate the complexity of the environment, and so they withdrew to avoid overstimulation. (Later we will discuss some of the neurological effects of the emergence from isolation.) Sackett (1968) adds support to our canid study in an experiment that he did with rhesus monkeys. He found that as rhesus monkeys get older they prefer to look at picture cards of increasing complexity. If monkeys are raised in isolation, at six months of age they prefer to look at cards of less complexity than those which rhesus monkeys normally prefer at that age. He concludes from these experiments that in the absence of paced increments of experience the organism will seek a lower level of stimulation and environmental complexity.

From these studies we may formulate an arousal-maintenance model of perceptual-motor homeostasis wherein the optimal arousal or tolerance level is "set" early in life as a result of the quality and quantity of early experiences. The level is set low in those animals that have had few increments of experience. If the environment does not provide varied stimulation, the subject may compensate by creating its own varied input by elaborating stereotyped motor acts or by directing specific activities toward inappro-

Normal and Abnormal Behavior Development

priate objects (such as copulating with its food bowl). The stereotyped motor acts (thumb-sucking, self-clutching, and rocking in primates) developed while in isolation may be performed when the subject is in a novel environment and may serve to reduce arousal or anxiety because they are familiar activities and may be comforting (Berkson, 1968). This type of stereotype is to be distinguished from the locomotor cage stereotypes described by Holzapfel (1968) which are derived from thwarted attempts to escape. Mason (1967) has developed a comparable theory in which he uses the term "general motivational state" in reference to the influence of the degree of arousal on the organization of behavior during different periods of development.

Social Isolation and Development

Mirsky (1968) draws the following conclusions from his studies of monkeys raised in isolation:

The data clearly indicated that the social isolation which had occurred during the first year of life of these now adult monkeys did not affect their capacity to acquire both discriminated instrumental and cardiac responses to avoidance stimuli. It did impair their ability to respond to social stimuli such as the facial expressions that communicated information regarding impending shock. Thus, they could neither express normally nor interpret accurately the social behavior of others of their species. Accordingly, it would appear that the ability to communicate effectively with other members of their species must be acquired by monkeys during early infancy, or not at all. This acquisition may be analogous to the phenomenon of "imprinting" or "primary socialization" described in other species. It is quite possible that the socially deprived monkey's inappropriate or deficient interpretation of nonverbal and other cues from other animals may account for the fact that normally reared monkeys ignore or avoid social isolates in preference to other normals. Dr. Mason and, more recently, Sackett have shown that a socially normal monkey detects, discriminates, and avoids isolates, thus further isolating them from the social group.

In reviewing their own studies of primates Jensen and Bobbitt (1968) show how the deprivation of inanimate play objects affects social behavior:

> Inanimate objects constitute another important class of environmental factors. Our tests of the effects of enrichment by toys indicate that lack of them and climbing facilities will seriously handicap the young animal in learning motor skills, in developing independence from its mother, and in interacting with peers. Further, these effects may be critical in determining later social dominance. We hypothesized that prior and concurrent toy experience facilitate peer socialization.

In an impoverished environment such as a barren cage there is a prolonged period of mother-infant closeness which is essentially a retardation in the mutual independence process. Mother-infant pairs in an enriched environment manipulate themselves and each other less and manipulate the environment more. Jensen and Bobbitt (1968) propose a continuous process of detachment of infant from mother (and vice versa) as attachments to the larger environment develop. Apparently deprived infants at six months of age are severely handicapped in social responsiveness when faced with an enriched peer, with respect to whom they are subordinate. These authors emphasize that short-term maternal separation or isolation from an enriched environment may actually intensify interaction when the infant is returned. This temporary increase in responsiveness after a brief period of separation (in effect, an instance where absence makes the heart grow fonder) clearly shows the importance of the duration of deprivation in addition to the type of deprivation and the age of the organism when deprivation occurs. Harlow (in Sackett, 1968) demonstrated

Normal and Abnormal Behavior Development

that prolonged social isolation can lead to severe impairment in social, sexual, and maternal behaviors later in life. He also discovered, however, that although an isolation-raised mother tends to reject her first offspring, her attitude toward subsequent offspring tends to be normal, provided she can be mated.

Another problem in the isolation-raised monkey is its failure to acquire the behavioral cues utilized by normal conspecifics. There is some evidence from G. Mitchell (personal communication) that the isolation-raised monkey gives an undifferentiated facial expression rather like the blank stare of a newborn human infant; he concludes that the isolate is in effect developmentally retarded. The infantile expression may resemble the direct threat stare of a normal mature adult, however, and therefore may release aggression when the animal is exposed to a normal monkey. It has also been shown that isolation-raised animals do not read the normal facial cues of conspecifics, and we can conclude therefore that although many displays are in fact innate, a great deal of learning and reinforcement is essential for their consolidation and integration into the normal behavior repertoire. Harlow is now attempting therapy of isolation-raised monkeys by providing them with infant monkeys, and the effects of the therapy appear to be extremely promising in bringing the isolate out of his self-directed, if not autistic, shell. A number of people have commented upon the similarities between the stereotypic and self-directed behaviors which develop in monkeys raised in isolation and comparable actions seen in autistic children; although the symptoms are remarkably similar, caution must be exercised in drawing such analogies.

Fuller (1967) has raised dogs in complete social isolation during early life and has demonstrated that genetic

FIG. 20. EEG recordings of a control pup and two isolation-raised pups on emergence from isolation. Note the bursts of spindlelike activity in the isolation-raised pups; this phenomenon disappeared as the hyperactive behavior of the subjects subsided. (From Fox, 1971b.)

differences have some bearing on the results. The relatively timid beagles were more affected by isolation than were the more aggressive and outgoing wirehaired terriers. Melzack and Scott (1957) isolated Scottish terriers and found that when these dogs were released from isolation they were not overcome with a mass fear response like Fuller's beagles but rather were hyperactive and similar in some ways to hyperkinetic children. They were extremely aroused and had a short attention span, shifting from one novel stimulus to another in a very disorganized fashion. They would also approach certain novel stimuli which normal dogs would avoid; for instance, they would repeatedly stick their noses into a candle flame. It was found that their response to

Normal and Abnormal Behavior Development

pain was impaired. The isolation subjects, for example, did not flinch when a needle was stuck through their skin. Work in our laboratory indicates that such impaired pain perception might be a result of the intense state of arousal in isolation-raised subjects when they are placed in a relatively novel environment. Four-week-old pups that were isolated for one week and then released were hyperactive and at the same time had an abnormal EEG (Figure 20) which contained spindlelike trains of fast frequency activity (Fox, 1971b). We also found that their evoked responses to visual stimulation were of significantly shorter latency than similar responses in the control animals. Within a few days, however, they recovered overtly—the latencies returned to normal, and the spindlelike activity in the EEG disappeared. There is a tentative correlation here between what seems to be an acute reticular arousal syndrome and the chronic reticular arousal syndrome in infantile autism as proposed by Hutt and his colleagues (1965).

In order for an organism to develop normally it would appear then that paced increments of experience are necessary for the normal exploratory drive to mature. If increments of experience are denied, the organism will prefer a less stimulating or less overloading environment. This concept is important in child-rearing and in education, for an understimulated child may eventually acquire a low set point for stimulation and complexity tolerance and may withdraw from any situations which cause undue overload. I believe that the entire basis for intelligence, for the acquisition of information, and for learning itself hinges upon early exploratory behavior; if the basic drive to explore is denied, then subsequent motivation to investigate, to manipulate the world, and consequently to learn will be greatly reduced.

Concepts in Ethology

Genetic and Family Influences

As in all developmental problems we must first consider the role of genetic factors. Henderson (1970) has elegantly demonstrated the interaction between genetic and environmental influences in the development of mice. Working with several strains, he found that the results with mice raised in enriched environments were somewhat similar to those obtained by Bennett and his colleagues (1964). The mice were superior to the controls raised under standard laboratory conditions in performance tests including various learning tasks and motivational tests of exploratory behavior. Henderson proposes that there is an environmental repression operating as a consequence of rearing under the relatively impoverished environment of the laboratory. He has also demonstrated that hybrids of the various mouse strains raised under standard laboratory conditions performed much better than the pure parent strains in various tests given to them at maturity (a typical example of hybrid vigor). When Henderson raised hybrids in enriched environments, their performance scores were also higher than those of pure strains that were raised under the same conditions. Henderson's paper is an important one for all people working with laboratory animals. (See also Fox, 1972a.)

Earlier in this book we have referred several times to the effects of child-rearing practices on the behavior of the maturing individual. Our best example of these effects in an animal model comes from the work of Kaufman and Rosenblum (1967) on pigtail and bonnet macaques. They found that when the mother of an infant bonnet macaque is removed from the colony, her infant is very little disturbed and is immediately accepted by other members of the group. When a pigtail mother is removed from the colony, her infant goes into a state of severe anaclitic depression and is not accepted or emotionally buffered by the group. The differences in the infants' reactions correlate with differences in maternal behavior. The pigtail mother is extremely possessive and does not allow other individuals close to her infant, whereas the bonnet mother is less possessive and allows conspecifics much freer access to her infant. Therefore we can conclude that a greater dependency develops between the mother and the offspring in pigtail macaques than in bonnet macaques. Anaclitic depression occurs when the symbiotic dependence of infant or mother is broken.

The effects of maternal deprivation and separation have been studied extensively in many laboratories, and it is beyond the scope and intent of this review to provide more than a brief overview. A considerable amount of literature has been published on the effects of maternal deprivation following the pioneer studies of Spitz (1949), Bowlby (1971), and Harlow (1965). Kaufman and Rosenblum (1967) have shown how the type of interaction bond established between mother and infant in monkeys influences the degree of separation depression that occurs when the infant is maternally deprived. Hinde and his colleagues (1966) have demonstrated that enduring effects are produced by even short-term separations of mother and infant. Mitchell (1970) has given an extensive review of such studies in primates and has also discussed the consequences of peer separation.

The "perpetual puppy" syndrome may develop in adult dogs if a symbiotic relationship has been maintained by overindulgent and permissive owners, and severe anaclitic depression may follow separation of the dogs from their owners for surgery, boarding, or quarantine (Fox, 1968). It should be emphasized that as a consequence of the symbiotic relationship with the owner the pet may develop a variety of care-soliciting (et-epimeletic) reactions such as whining, jumping up, following constantly throughout the house, crying when left alone, and submissive urination. These symptoms resemble regression in man to more neotenous or infantile behaviors. Punishment after the disturbed pet (or child) has urinated, defecated, or generally pestered the owner sufficiently may be a masochistic form of reinforcement.

"Sympathy" lameness, hysterical paraplegia, and coxalgia have been described in dogs (Fox, 1968) and are well documented in man as attention-seeking reactions. Chess (1969) stresses the correlation between acute illness and dependency behavior in human infants. After recovery the child attempts to maintain the interpersonal relationship that brought him special attention during the illness. Some overindulged pets have been known to refuse to use one limb after surgery for congenital patella luxation because they received so much attention and petting from their owners while they were recovering. In extreme cases, muscle atrophy developed; in others, surgical recovery was complete, but the subjects would suddenly become lame when they were in an anxiety or conflict-provoking situation and were soliciting the attention of their owners. (We should also keep in mind the genetic acquisition of comparable reactions in certain animals, notably the sham death or tonic immobility of many species and the hysterical hemiplegia or the sham broken wing displayed by ground-nesting birds such as the ringed plover to distract predators.)

In this chapter we have discussed the three levels of stimulation that affect development: first, visceral or autonomic stimulation associated with early handling stress;

FIG. 21. Schema of relationships between stages of development of the central nervous system and the times when various types of environmental influence have their greatest effect. *1.* Handling early in life affects the adrenal-pituitary, autonomic, and reticular activating systems. *2.* Development of social attachments correlates with the development of limbic (emotional) centers. *3.* Social and environmental influences affect brain maturation.

second, limbic emotional stimulation associated with socialization; and third, a cortical level of stimulation associated with environmental enrichment or deprivation (Figure 21). We find that development must be considered not as a linear progression but rather as a complex series of interactions leading to levels of greater complexity through developmental stages, through a series of critical and sensitive periods, and through other periods involving structural and functional integration. As mentioned in the first chapter, neoteny, a principle involving prolonged infancy and a plastic "open system" kind of neural apparatus, makes man a virtually unique species.

The knowledge that is being gained from comparative developmental studies in human and nonhuman animals could lead us to the point where we can in fact provide programmed life histories for rearing infants in order to optimize their potentials. We will not be producing super-organisms, but rather we will be reinforcing what is latent in their genetic repertoire by ensuring that the developing phenotype will be as adaptive as possible to predictable future conditions and that it will also be flexible and modifiable. Early handling regimes can influence emotional stability, learning ability, and resistance or susceptibility to psychological stress and diseases; they might also have some interaction effect in the efficacy of vaccination programs and in immune responses. In addition, we must consider the overall importance of socialization in facilitating the integration of individuals into society and, more broadly, in harmonizing different cultures throughout the world to promote global peace and unity. Finally, we must consider also the intellectual and creative abilities that might be nurtured by provision of the right kind of varied stimulation during early life.

CHAPTER *4*

APPLIED ETHOLOGY

Ethology and Animal Science

The livestock owner, the husbandryman, the grazier, the herdsman, the shepherd, and the farmer have all developed "informal" principles—some traditional, some superstitious, some the product of trial and error—which they apply in their everyday handling of animals. Although much of their knowledge is based upon experience, part of it is usually redundant if not actually incorrect. It would be difficult for the average student in veterinary science or agricultural science to acquire this large body of informal knowledge and even more difficult for him to sort out that which is valuable and sound from that which is a product of tradition and superstition. If he could do so, however, he would certainly be a superior graduate who would have to do far less "unlearning" of what he has learned from the textbooks on the basis of what he finds in the reality of practice. Ethology can help to bridge this gap by providing the student with the basic principles of animal behavior; the relevance of ethology to veterinary medicine

NOTE: This chapter is based on a lecture in the Wesley W. Spink Lectures on Comparative Medicine presented at the University of Minnesota, Minneapolis campus, on October 19, 1973. The content is derived in part from information in Klinghammer and Fox (1971). See also Bryant (1972).

and its general place in undergraduate science education have been discussed at length elsewhere (Fox, 1967; 1973b). The application of ethological principles in animal science can also suggest improved methods of maintaining domesticated animals, which in turn could contribute to economic gain.

With these practical considerations in mind, let us now turn to a number of issues that are relevant to the applied science of ethology. A fundamental question should be posed at this juncture, namely, What is normal behavior for a given domestic species under the conditions in which it is kept? To determine a normal behavioral baseline for socially isolated hybrid battery hens or close-penned veal calves is difficult. Behavior is a product—the phenotype, if you wish—of a series of genotype-environment interactions to which the organism is exposed during its development. First, in many hybrids and special utility strains of domesticated animals we must recognize the effect of artificial selection on the gene pool of a given population. This selective modification may be designed to emphasize rapid growth, the persistence of the infantile characteristics of neoteny, or the repression of the development of mature features such as thick skin and heavy bones, or it may be directed toward earlier sexual maturity, high fertility, heavy lactation, or tolerance for the close proximity of others (low aggression). Consequently, changes have occurred in the endocrine system and the behavior patterns of these animals, making them quite different from their wild counterparts and from randomly bred multipurpose strains and breeds. Second, the emerging phenotype may be further modified by routine practices initiated early in its development (castration, hormone implants, food additives, high protein diet, disbudding of calves' horns, removal of boars' tusks, and ringing of pigs to prevent rooting). Finally, behavior may be modified further by the conditions under which the animals are raised (in closed social groups of one sex, in separate pens under varying degrees of social and sensory deprivation, or in communal pens under relatively crowded conditions). Thus, in deciding what baseline is normal for a given animal, we must consider the effects of domestication, differences in genotype, and the methods of husbandry employed.

A number of routine practices in animal husbandry are based upon ethological principles which have been experimentally tested under controlled laboratory conditions. For instance, the role of olfactory stimuli in the sexual behavior of farm animals has been studied in this way. At artificial insemination (A-I) centers the donor animals are conditioned to the use of a dummy model sow or cow. In Germany it has been found that a boar will more readily mount a dummy that has been "spiced" with the vaginal pheromone of an estrous sow, and semen production may be increased. Similarly, a sow will stand better for artificial insemination if she is exposed to the boar's natural odors. But problems can and do arise in A-I centers where bulls, lacking the sociosexual stimulation of having a herd of females around, may refuse to mount the dummy; because they seem to lose their libido, they produce less sperm. (Social and sexual rehabilitation is easily effected by putting the bull out to pasture with a few cows for a short time.)

Another intriguing role played by olfactory stimuli is in the imprinting of a ewe or a mare to her offspring. Imprinting is a phenomenon that is little understood but well recognized among husbandrymen, and it has received a great deal of attention by ethologists (Sluckin, 1965; Klinghammer, 1967). The husbandryman is aware of the problems encountered in getting a mare or a ewe to accept an orphan. With horses the usual practice is to sponge up the sweat and sebaceous materials of the mare, especially from the udder, and to wipe them onto the orphan foal. This greatly reduces the probability of its being rejected. If a ewe's lamb has died, it is common practice to skin it and to put the skin over an orphan lamb or one of another ewe's twins and give it to her. Rejection is rare under such circumstances, Few shepherds bother to bottle-raise an orphan lamb because it will invariably become attached to people and at a later age may not join up with the flock. In Australia "placer" lambs are also destroyed because they will not stay with the flock; these lambs apparently become imprinted upon a particular place (such as the spot where the mother died) and not onto the foster mother.

Another area where the husbandryman uses certain principles of ethology is in the handling and restraint of animals. When an animal is held or touched in a particular region of the body, it can be restrained with very little force. In the dog seizure of the scruff or the muzzle and contact with the groin or the inguinal area are effective. These regions are associated with intraspecific contact during aggressive and social or investigative interaction, during which the subordinate individual remains passive. Man similarly asserts dominance in handling a dog when he makes appropriate contact with these "psychologically" significant body regions (Fox, 1971a). In farm animals, however, the patterns of dominance and subordination are not so strong, and physical contact with certain body regions is effective for other reasons. Stroking and scratching the withers of a horse have a calming effect on the animal because it is this region that horses nuzzle and groom.

Applied Ethology

Many methods of restraining farm animals are based upon the natural tendency of animals to remain still when turned over—the tonic immobility or catatonic reaction—which is seen especially in poultry and sheep. In horses placing a twitch around the ear or the nose—and in cattle seizing the muzzle with pincers and ringing the nose—or simply picking up one foot will effectively immobilize the animal so that a number of routine procedures can be undertaken. Bandaging the eyes is very effective in horses, and of course in falcons and hawks the technique of hooding has been employed for centuries. In sows rubbing the udder and the inguinal region has a marked quieting effect. In cattle the udder-cinch (a noose passed around the abdomen and pulled tight just in front of the udder) and the technique of pinching the skin in the mid-lumbar region (Ewbank, 1968) can be used effectively to immobilize the animal. Contact in these areas may be related to udder contact by a calf or a subordinate cow and to flank and dorsum contact by the bull during copulation.

Another method used to control sheep and cattle rests upon the fact that they are herd animals which tend to follow each other and, as a group, to follow a leader (an older ewe or "bellwether" or an older cow). This greatly facilitates the handling of large numbers of animals since the group-coordinated behavior of the species can be channeled appropriately to induce the animals to go in a particular direction. The herdsman is always careful not to overstimulate the animals, for a panic flight reaction might be triggered. A somewhat novel stimulus such as a cattle crush may be very disturbing to the animals, and many dairymen leave the crush close to the dairy yard so the animals can become accustomed to it. Ewbank (1968) studied the behavior of cattle in a squeeze pen and found that the order of their entry into the crush is related to social dominance.

Husbandrymen are well aware that animals and poultry may be injured as a result of a panic reaction. In the breeding of turkeys there has been careful genetic selection of hybrid strains that do not panic easily. Chicken houses are often designed without corners where the floor and walls intersect so that if the birds are panicked by a sudden noise they cannot pile themselves into corners, crushing or injuring a number of birds in the process. A constantly maintained level of noise or background music may serve as a sound curtain to reduce the possibility of panic from sudden noises.

Several operant and classical conditioning procedures are used in animal husbandry, ranging from the dairyman calling in the cows at a set time for milking (they eventually start moving toward the milking parlor at the right time without needing to be called) to the clanging of milking equipment which prompts the cows to "let down" the milk. A number of operant devices—for instance, those which require the animal to press a lever to receive water or food—can be utilized by pigs and cattle.

Husbandrymen know that by modifying the physical environment of their animals they can often increase production. Improved ventilation can make it possible to house more animals per cubic foot. The use of partitions to segregate animals singly or in closed social groups also allows more individuals to be housed under the same roof. Social distance is therefore increased between groups, and the deleterious consequences of crowding stress are reduced. Behavior and endocrine activity in chickens can be controlled effectively by appropriate design of the battery unit. A hen is an indeterminate layer; if it sits on the eggs that

Applied Ethology

it has laid, it will stop laying. The trap-nesting technique, in which the egg is removed as soon as it is laid, keeps the bird laying and prevents it from becoming broody. Egg production is enhanced further by altering the circadian rhythm (an increase in day length increases the yield of eggs).

The social hierarchy—the pecking order in poultry and the bunting order in cattle—is another factor in the behavior of farm animals and often has indirect economic implications. It is unlikely that the husbandryman is in the dominant or alpha position as is the usual rule in the relationship between man and dog. In closed social groups of animals a clear social hierarchy exists in which each individual knows his place, and fighting over food, mates, or status is therefore reduced. If the group is enclosed in a very limited space, however, social disorganization and fighting may ensue. Subordinates are the first to suffer from such crowding stress; the growth rate is reduced and adrenal hypertrophy follows, coupled with decreased resistance to disease, lowered lactation, and infertility. Nevertheless, in the domestication process there must already have been considerable selection for resistance to crowding stress or at least some selection for low aggressivity and tolerance for close proximity of conspecifics. Pigs, for example, are relatively tolerant of crowded conditions, but tail-biting and outbreaks of secondary clostridial or Fusiformis infections which lower weight gain do occur. Cannibalism, feather-pecking, and eye-pecking in poultry are often attributable to crowding stress; one alpha individual who remains unscathed can usually be identified as the immediate source of the trouble. Even when there is adequate space, the addition of new poultry or cattle to an established social group causes social disorganization which persists until a new hierarchy is set up. During the interim production in terms of milk yield or weight gain may be drastically reduced.

There are many aspects of agricultural science which could benefit from ethological studies. These can be divided into four major economically pertinent categories. First, fertility, reproductive competence, and maternal adequacy may be influenced by social and environmental factors such as crowding stress and relative social deprivation. Second, productivity in terms of growth rate and weight gain may also be affected by social and environmental factors. Third, the inheritance of desirable and undesirable traits and their phenotypic development may vary under different rearing and maintenance regimes. Finally, having identified and analyzed those factors that influence productivity, the interaction effects of strain or genotype with animal husbandry methods (the artificial "ecology" of farm animals) should be explored to determine how they increase or decrease susceptibility to psychophysiological stress, infections, and metabolic disease.

As we will discuss at some length later in this section, one of the most critical issues today is the standardization of animals for research not only in terms of nutrition and disease control but also in terms of genetics, the effects of early experience, and the effects of the social and physical environment in which the animals are kept (Fox, 1972a). Identification, control, and international standardization of such variables are essential, for the quality of the laboratory animals available today rarely meets the optimum standards for use in biomedical research. Laboratory studies in the area of psychobiology must be supported by more field studies of animals in their natural habitat to verify and to supplement laboratory findings and also to provide essential

Applied Ethology

information about the optimal conditions for the rearing and maintenance of animals in captivity.

A few points relative to the propagation of zoo animals should also be mentioned. Reference has already been made to the problems of hand-raising animals, which often becomes necessary because the mother might neglect or kill her offspring for various reasons (Holzapfel, 1968). It is possible that in some species we are gradually selecting against and eliminating normal maternal behavior. For example, Japanese quail have been raised artificially in brooders for generations because the adult females are notoriously lacking in maternal behavior. Will the zoos in the year 2,000 be propagating and conserving many species by artificial insemination and hand-rearing? We should decide now whether we want to avert this and, if so, what steps to take. Certainly we should spend more effort in studying the environmental requirements of captive species (including laboratory animals) as pleaded by Hediger (1950) and Fox (1972a). According to Morris (1966), some species (neophilic species) have a higher requirement for varied stimulation and opportunities to explore and manipulate than others (neophobic species). Perhaps we should also vigorously cull specimens that would not survive in nature because they are genetically or phenotypically inferior. The environment in which animals are raised and exhibited is of both humane and practical concern. The animals in many zoos are kept in environments which are impoverished in terms of their general structure and complexity and which do not supply the animals with objects to manipulate, work or activities to perform (Hediger, 1950), and conspecifics with which to interact. In other instances the animals suffer from crowded conditions. Morris (1966) and Fox (1972a) have discussed these problems in detail as they relate to both zoo and laboratory animals.

Ethology and Laboratory Animals

The purpose of this section is to focus attention on a number of environmental factors that affect the behavior of laboratory animals. Such environmental factors may constitute highly significant experimental variables; if these factors are not recognized and controlled, the significance of the experimental data may be questionable. The environmental variables in laboratory animal husbandry include cage size and type; population density per cage and per room; sex distribution per cage and per room; distribution of species per room; provision for exercise; availability of environmental stimulation; methods of rearing, handling, and socialization; and factors related to caretakers and handlers. In addition there are the effects of temperature, humidity, sound, and deodorants; the stresses of transportation, quarantine, and conditioning or "shaping" to the laboratory animal facility; and the influence of circadian rhythms. All of these factors, along with the effects of general care, obviously must enter into any discussion of the most humane conditions under which to develop and maintain suitable laboratory animals.

Behavior in response to change may be overt in terms of activity or maintenance functions (such as eating) and may bring about further physiological or pathological changes within the animal. Laboratory animal ethology might be defined as the objective study of behavior under laboratory and experimental conditions. Any social, environmental, or endocrine change may influence the health and well-being of the animal and detract from its value as a subject for experimentation. A number of areas of concern, such as the effects on rodents of deodorants or of cage position, have not been investigated. It is hoped that by pointing out areas where there is a deficiency of knowledge this section may supply the impetus for further investigation of these aspects of laboratory animal care. Our dual objectives therefore are to give the investigator an awareness of behaviorally derived variables which may affect his experiment and to provide recommendations for animal health from the ethological point of view.

There has been considerable discussion about how representative laboratory animals are of their wild counterparts. Genetic selection, either controlled or inadvertent, and the unnatural ecologies and intrinsic environmental and experiential variables to which laboratory animals are subjected, have produced animals very different from those in nature. We should be aware of the differences that occur in laboratory-propagated animals, and the process of "laboratorification" deserves very careful and continued analysis in both inbred and wild-caught animals. Richter (1954) emphasized that the laboratory rat is relatively hypergonadal and hypoadrenal compared to its wild counterpart, and such endocrine changes stem from artificial selection for high fertility and docility.

It is known that overcrowding or confinement of animals in a limited space increases the frequency of social interactions and interrupts ongoing behaviors; it can also cause an increase in territorial fighting and may give rise to Selye's stress syndrome, especially in subordinates. The aggression that follows overcrowding in wild populations regulates the population as a feedback mechanism via the adrenal-pituitary axis (Christian and Davis, 1964). Since laboratory animals are typically housed under crowded conditions, one biological consequence of "laboratorification" may have been selection for proximity tolerance, low aggressivity, and consequently resistance to crowding stress. Along these lines Marsden and Bronson (1964), for example, have found that the Bruce effect (the blocking of pregnancy in a recently inseminated female mouse by exposure to a strange male) cannot be demonstrated in highly inbred mouse strains, although it operates in wild house mice (*Mus musculus*) and in deer mice. Even brief recurrent stimulation such as occasional moving of the cage by the attendant can block pregnancy in wild mice during the first forty-eight hours after insemination. The fact that this general arousal or alarm effect is not seen in inbred laboratory mice emphasizes the great autonomic and endocrine differences in reactivity between wild and laboratory subspecies. Clearly "laboratorification" has influenced the social and sexual behavior and the endocrine functions of many strains of laboratory animals, and these changes may in turn influence the results of experiments.

Another point that should be raised is the possible deleterious effect of suboptimal stress (overswaddling) in the rearing and maintenance of laboratory animals. For example, if mother rats are regularly removed from the nest for short periods, there is a demonstrable effect upon the emotional reactivity of the young, comparable to the effect of early handling, which makes them less emotional and more resistant to a variety of stresses later in life (Morton, 1968). In nature the young would normally be exposed to a variety of mild stresses such as being left alone for varying periods while the mother is out foraging for food. Experiments might therefore be designed to include one group of animals that have been exposed to a standardized regime of handling early in life. The inclusion of such environmental and experiential variables, when carefully controlled, could add greatly to the relevance of toxicological assays and immunological research.

Bennett and his colleagues (1964) and others have demonstrated marked structural and biochemical changes in the brain and the existence of behavioral (learning) deficits in rats raised in complete social isolation compared to rats raised in an enriched environment in which they were in social groups and had access to numerous play objects. Rats raised under standard laboratory conditions showed deficits similar to those of the isolation-raised rats. In other words it has been shown that the genetic capacity or potential for brain and behavior development can be influenced by the environment. We may now ask how near normality, or how representative of a normal population, are those uniform rats that have been propagated for generations in the impoverished, sterile environment of the "standard" cage. Other laboratory species have not as yet undergone the same degree of behavioral modification as a consequence of "laboratorification" (Kavanau, 1964). But we should take heed of the findings on rats and recognize the possibility that comparable changes may be brought about in carnivores, primates, and other species that are selectively bred and raised solely for laboratory use.

Unlike other laboratory species, the cat and more especially the dog have been subjected to thousands of years of domestication. This has resulted in marked structural and behavioral changes (and idiosyncrasies) compared to their wild ancestors and has also introduced some degree of neoteny or perseverance of infantile characteristics (Fox, 1971a). The behavioral changes that occur in primates as a consequence of artificial selection in an artificial environment have yet to be identified, but the present methods of rearing and propagating primates should be thoroughly reviewed to determine the fitness of the laboratory environment for the optimization of development and to identify suboptimal conditions (space restriction, abnormal social grouping, and social and experiential deprivation) which may have deleterious consequences.

A rational and scientifically sound plan for the propagation of research animals (and also zoo stock) would be to breed and raise certain species in natural or seminatural enclosures. This would be feasible and very economical for rodents, lagomorphs, caviemorphs, carnivores, and primates. They might be randomly or line-colony bred and socialized to handlers early in life; these animals could be used widely for experimental purposes except in those few studies where highly inbred and mutant genetic models are required. In the past we have tended to exhibit an "edifice complex"—a fondness for expensive buildings with internal environmental controls and carefully designed space requirements (which frequently become inadequate shortly after construction is completed)—in the maintenance and propagation of research animals. It is true that for research areas such as immunology carefully controlled environmental conditions are essential for the production of gnotobiotic and SPF (specific pathogen free) stock, but for many research areas feral or naturally raised stock would be adequate if not preferable and certainly would be less costly. In addition, the judicious setting aside of "reserve areas" for the maintenance and production of various species would be a safeguard against the extinction of some species (particularly primates) in their natural habitats. In this connection many countries have already imposed export restrictions to control the depletion of certain indigenous species. This in itself should persuade scientists to consider seriously the practicality of reserve areas which would ensure an adequate supply of research animals and simultaneously would eliminate both the present risk of importing diseased stock and the heavy losses of animals that frequently occur as a result of careless management after capture and during exportation.

A second rational and scientifically sound proposal would be to investigate the consequences and potentials of raising laboratory animals under various regimes of programmed life histories as suggested by Denenberg and Whimbey (1963). Scheduled handling stress, socialization, and environmental and experiential enrichment could be instituted in both laboratory animal facilities and zoos. Furthermore, laboratory animal facilities should emphasize the ecological and behavioral requirements of the animals instead of forcing the animals to adapt to conditions imposed upon them for the convenience of handlers and research personnel (Figure 22). This would reduce the possibility that aspects of behavior and normal physiological functions might inadvertently be modified to the detriment of the animal and its future offspring and eventually to the detriment of the experiment.

BEHAVIORAL CONSIDERATIONS
IN ROUTINE EXPERIMENTAL PROCEDURES

A number of unstandardized procedures are used routinely in a variety of experiments with animals. As yet, many of these procedures have not been investigated to assess the degree to which they may constitute untoward experimental variables. For example, one particular method of restraint may be superior for a given species because the degree of arousal and sympathetic adrenal reaction (which may alter hematocrit values or some dependent physiological

FIG. 22. Schema of adaptation to captivity. *A, B.* Critical stress phase. *B, C.* Transitional adaptation phase. Not all animals reach phase C, especially if they are fully mature when captured. Over successive generations artificial selection to standardize the phenotypes characteristic of phase C may eventually alter the wild genotype so that the gene pool of the captive colony is atypical because it has been modified and adapted to an unnatural environment. Foundation animals that reach phase C are more likely than others to breed in captivity, and their reproductive rate is an important selector for a genotype that more closely approximates the adapted phenotype. Where adaptation involves innate or genetic capacity rather than early experience or socialization, such a selection process is highly probable.

variable) may be less than that resulting from other methods of restraint.

Transport and caging. Some time should be allowed for animals to settle down both behaviorally and metabolically after they have been transported any distance. If transportation also results in a drastic change in the animal's environment (for instance, when a wild-caught monkey is brought into the laboratory or a kennel-reared dog is placed in a metabolism cage), the animal may require a long conditioning or adaptation period before it attains sufficient stability to permit experimentation. In addition, a change in social relationships might also require some period of adaptation or compensation. Group-reared rats, dogs, or monkeys that are placed in separate cages have to adapt to social isolation or deprivation; this may be extremely stressful for some social species such as the rhesus macaque and especially for young animals which are separated from their mothers. Conversely, putting new animals together or either removing resident individuals or introducing new individuals into an established social group results in a new social environment, and some time should be allowed for social reorganization to occur. Finally, the experimenter should bear in mind that "random" seizure of animals from a group cage may not actually be random; he may in fact be selecting out individuals that are less active, less emotional (or more emotional), or perhaps even blind, deaf, or sick.

Feeding and housekeeping. Routine procedures such as feeding and watering the animals, cleaning the cages, and putting the animals back into the clean cages should be considered in relation to the timing of the experiment. A break in the routine or a change in the time when routine procedures are conducted may have some influence on experimentation. The investigator has to consider carefully factors such as how long before or after feeding or cleaning he should begin his experiment. A full stomach influences body weight, and indirectly it can interfere, for example, with the effectiveness of anesthesia or the dose of drug per unit of body weight in a toxicological study. A change of bedding may increase activity in some laboratory species, especially rodents. It is difficult for investigators studying the effects of handling, for example, to convince animal supervisors that the cages of the animals involved must not be cleaned out in the usual way. In these studies the type of cage is important: rats in cages with wire-mesh floors receive less handling than do rats in cages with solid floors which have to be cleaned more frequently. In some rodent colonies cage positions are changed in order to control for "position effects" that might result from the fact that the rodents on the lowest tier of cages have a very different microclimate and possibly less social contact with the caretaker than those at higher levels. Cage rotation dilutes such effects by providing each rat with a similar range of experiential and microenvironmental variation.

In general, because the extraneous variables have not been fully identified and their influence on many experiments has not been verified, investigators tend to adhere to a set routine. Experiments may begin, say, one hour after feeding or cage cleaning. Such arbitrary standardization reduces the possibility of observing the increased variability in results which might occur if the subjects were studied at widely different times before or after cage cleaning or feeding. The mere rattling of a pencil across a rat's cage can produce a measurable adreno-sympathetic response.

In most rodent colonies and in many colonies of dogs and primates food and water are available at all times, and the replenishment of feed hoppers and the installation of fresh water bottles are done on a regular basis. In a few instances the animal itself is able to control its supplies of food and water, which are dispensed when the animal performs some operant task such as licking or pushing a bar. These automated devices make it possible to keep a very precise record of food and water intake for each separately caged animal. On ad-lib or self-regulated regimes most animals maintain a fairly regular intake, which is organized into bouts of feeding and drinking superimposed upon the daily circadian activity rhythm.

Caretaker effects. In order to control for the caretaker effect which develops when one part of the animal colony is routinely tended by one person, it may be considered advantageous to rotate personnel on a day-to-day basis from one part of the colony to another. This is satisfactory,

Applied Ethology

provided of course that all personnel follow a set pattern of cleaning, feeding, and handling. The rotation method will prevent the animals from becoming overly attached or habituated to one particular person and will make them generally easier to handle by various caretakers and by the experimenter and his technician. McCall, Lester, and Corter (1969) have demonstrated in rats a preference for the caretakers who raised them, the preference being mediated by olfactory cues. Caretaker rotation would help to prevent such preferences from developing.

Exercise and environmental stimulation. The importance of exercise in maintaining good physical and "mental" condition in laboratory animals has not been evaluated thoroughly. Different breeds of dogs show marked differences in daily activity (Burns and Fraser, 1966) and may therefore have different exercise or activity requirements. Dogs with a low requirement for activity are preferred for the laboratory. It is not known if exercise or physical activity per se is behaviorally beneficial; for instance, behavioral benefit from exercise on a treadmill is doubtful since this activity represents an abnormal stereotype. What may be especially beneficial to dogs is social contact with companions of their own species or with caretakers and freedom to explore an interesting environment. Under these circumstances exercise or activity occurs as a natural consequence of social interaction or exploration.

Varied stimulation can be made available to confined animals by allowing them visual contact with companions in opposite cages and by providing them with objects to manipulate. Leash-trained dogs might be walked around the animal facility and exposed to audio-visual stimuli of varying intensity and complexity. This would be especially advantageous and appropriate in long-term experiments during which the subject has to adapt to a new set of complex and novel stimuli. Too often an animal assigned to a particular experimental treatment experiences a decrement in attention or a shift to a new regime of attention, which can introduce undesirable experimental variables.

In general it is a poor policy to begin an experiment before an animal has fully adjusted to isolation from cage-mates, less human contact, a change of handler, new handling procedures, or confinement in a smaller cage. We lack data about the effects of these changes on physiological measures and the period of shaping or conditioning that is necessary before experimentation. It may be argued that such caution is excessive if control animals are also used, but this has not been tested. We must consider the possibility that deleterious interaction of emotional stressors could result in an additive effect capable of making measures of dependent variables quite erroneous. Long-term experimentation while an animal is adapting to the new environmental milieu is also questionable. The values of the dependent variables may change as a consequence of general adaptation rather than as a response of the organism to experimentation. Clearly the investigator must ensure that the animal has adapted and is physiologically stable, and, if possible, should collect some normal baseline readings before treatment so that the animal serves to some extent as its own control.

Circadian variables. All animals show changes in almost every physiological and behavioral parameter measured during a twenty-four-hour period. These circadian phenomena vary among nocturnal, diurnal, and crepuscular species, and they are influenced by external factors such as the ratio of daylight to darkness. In view of the fact that changes in temperature and humidity have a tonic effect while changes in illumination have a phasic, circadian effect, perhaps making temperature and humidity uniform in the laboratory might be as deleterious to some species as maintaining the animals in total darkness or under constant illumination. Since estrus in many animals is photoperiodic, an unvarying ratio of daylight to darkness may also influence fertility and other as yet unmeasured parameters.

The quality of light provided for laboratory animals may also influence behavior and endocrine function. The only available artificial lighting that has spectral qualities similar to those of sunlight (including a low-level emission of ultraviolet light) is the Vitalite produced by the Durotest Corporation. Preliminary findings from zoos and laboratory animal facilities that have used this type of artificial illumination are very promising.

To reduce the variability of results and to control for these circadian phenomena, most investigators begin experimentation at the same time every day. But is it the best, the most appropriate time of day to study a particular variable? The animal's metabolism or the activity of a particular enzyme system may be at its highest or lowest phase in the circadian cycle. The effectiveness of a drug or an experimental procedure or the animal's resistance to a toxin or infection may be quite different at, say, 8:00 A.M. and 4:00 P.M. In other words, to adhere blithely to a fixed time schedule may mask circadian variables which might alter the entire significance of the results, if not the validity of the experiment itself. Although researchers in some laboratories still do their experiments on rats at an hour that is virtually in the middle of the night for rats, many others now have controlled light-dark cycles in their animal facilities and use red light (which may or may not have some effects itself on nocturnal animals) during the workday.

Finally, a word about the "Monday morning" syndrome. After a quiet weekend many animal facilities are turned upside down every Monday when the cages are cleaned and prepared for weekly sterilization. A few alterations in work schedules (especially those for cage sterilization) so that a few cages are done every day, for example, instead of all at once would eliminate the weekend lull and the "Monday morning" syndrome. Designing animal facilities so that the animals are kept in small room-colonies would also reduce the intense and extended disturbance of weekly cleaning in a very large room-colony.

Handling and restraint. Primates can be moved from their home cages into a transportation cage for the journey to the laboratory or the testing room with a minimum of physical and psychological trauma if the animals first become accustomed to entering the transportation cage for food. These cages, which can be attached to the home pen, open and close with a guillotine door. Without proper equipment chaos can result, for instance, when attendants enter a colony cage of primates and try to catch one; if the animals are kept singly in cages, the job is much more easily accomplished. In cages with double fronts the movable inner section can be used as a vertical crush to restrain individual animals against the rear wall. This method is expedient and probably the least traumatic way of restraining unsocialized primates for simple procedures such as giving injections or taking blood samples.

Handling and restraint of cats and dogs are greatly facilitated if the animals have been socialized by frequent human contact earlier in life. A cat that has been caught

Applied Ethology

in a net or a dog that has been snared around the throat is in a poor physiological and psychological state. Such procedures are usually reserved for emergency treatment, although some investigators continue to use wild, intractable, and unsocialized animals for research studies which in turn may be prejudiced at the outset by variables that are a consequence of rough handling of the animals during capture and restraint.

Restraint during some experimental procedures is an extremely important interphase between the experimenter, the animal, and the handler. Inadequate restraint may allow the animal to struggle, and as a result excessive sympathetic adrenal arousal may significantly alter a number of parameters that might be studied in a blood sample. Excessive arousal of the animal while it is restrained can also result in its sudden collapse or its hyperexcitability during the induction of anesthesia. All people who are to work with experimental animals need some formal instruction on the best methods of restraint and handling; they will also improve through trial and error, but their errors may jeopardize the value of an experiment. Thorough training with different species and with individual animals that differ in temperament (which is especially relevant when working with dogs) is an important part of the animal handler's education.

With unsocialized and nondomesticated animals (especially primates) one may have to resort to judo techniques or to hardware such as crush cages or restraining chairs. The latter are used when prolonged studies are being undertaken, and it is imperative that the subjects become completely familiarized and adapted or "shaped" to the chair and the ancillary equipment before the experiment is started. Conscious dogs, cats, rabbits, and rodents are frequently secured by their legs on horizontal restraining tables; such treatment is inhumane and extremely stressful to the animal. Rats restrained in this way may develop gastric ulcers within a few hours.

Some species which are occasionally used in the laboratory can be restrained by "hooding" (a traditional practice in falconry). Other species (rats, rabbits, and chickens) can be induced into a state of tonic immobility or cataplexy by various procedures; some handlers are very adept at this. With socialized dogs and cats rhythmic stimulation by petting with a free hand and talking in a gentle voice are effective in quieting a tense or struggling animal. The same is true for horses. There is an extensive literature on the methods of restraint that may be used with various laboratory and domesticated species, and it would be superfluous to review them here. A few remarks in the light of behavioral observations, however, are relevant.

In the cat seizure of the scruff normally causes an inhibition of movement: this occurs naturally when the mother carries her kitten or when the male mounts and immobilizes the female by seizing the nape of her neck before intromission. It is no accident therefore that cats are quite easily restrained once they are firmly grasped at the back of the neck. It is also safe to apply pressure as necessary to hold the cat down because it is difficult for the animal to bite the handler from this position. It is more of a problem to restrain the claws, but an effective procedure is to seize the cat around the scruff and lumbar region (the base of the tail) and place its feet on a wire mesh or cloth surface. It will then dig its claws in, in a sense redirecting its aggressive clawing away from the handler. A similar procedure is used to secure less tractable

Applied Ethology

rats and mice. The tail is seized with forceps or one hand and the animal is lifted onto the wire mesh of its cage. As soon as it digs in its claws and attempts to run off, the handler slightly increases the tension on the animal's tail and runs his other hand down its back until he is able to get a secure hold on the scruff of its neck. If the tension on the tail suddenly gives way, the handler will know that the animal's feet are free, and he may then be bitten if he has not yet secured a good scruff hold.

A scruff hold is also effective with dogs, but it is often unnecessary. If the dog is reasonably tractable, the handler may place one arm under the dog's neck and hold the animal close to him, the other hand being free to hold the muzzle, groin or inguinal region, or forelimb for injection purposes. The muzzle hold, or muzzling with tape, will effectively subdue an aggressive or unpredictable dog. Seizing and closing a conspecific's muzzle is part of ritualized aggression in canids and appears to be an effective means of asserting psychological dominance over a dog. Touching the groin or inguinal region is a social gesture in dogs; the subordinate individual allows the dominant one to initiate it and remains passive or inhibited during contact. Most socialized dogs become quite passive when the handler gently places the palm of one hand in the inguinal fold.

The animal handler has to acquire some ethological knowledge; he must be able to "read" the nonverbal signals of his animals and to assess what emotional state they are in and how they are likely to react to him. He should be able to predict what an animal might do by being alert for warning signals, intention movements, and so on. He must also learn how much physical force is required in conjunction with the appropriate restraining holds. Dogs and cats struggle if they are held too tightly, but they begin to relax when properly restrained; if the handler also begins to relax, however, he may suddenly find that he has been bitten or that the animal has escaped.

OTHER FACTORS AFFECTING EXPERIMENTAL VARIABLES

Other factors and routine procedures which may influence experimental variables and which should be taken into account by the investigator include litter composition, weaning, marking for identification purposes, and postsurgical care.

Litter composition. Differences in litter size in multiparous mammals such as rodents and carnivores may be a potential source of experimental variability. Small litters are nutritionally and metabolically quite different from larger litters and show differences in growth rate, social organization, and behavior (for instance, in competitiveness). The mothers (rats or dogs) behave differently toward large litters, and such reactions could in turn affect the phenotype of the offspring. In order to partially control for these variables, it is a good practice to reduce the litter size in rodents to eight or ten pups and to discard litters of fewer than six unless they can be increased in number by adding a few pups from a larger litter of the same age. Such cross-fostering, especially between strains, may also affect the phenotype and should therefore be limited to cross-fostering within strains. The absence of a male in a group of female rodents not only influences their reproductive cycles but can delay sexual maturity (Vandenbergh, 1969), so the age and sex composition of social groups should also be considered. Finally, animals in groups show strong allelomimetic or group-coordinated activities (for instance, pups housed in groups tend to eat more), and this might also have an effect on experimental data.

Applied Ethology

Weaning. The optimal time for weaning varies between species and between breeds or strains. Experimenters usually allow weaning to proceed naturally in primates, cats, and dogs; in some instances this may be extremely traumatic for the young because for various reasons the mother may threaten and attack them (especially at feeding time in dogs, for example), and hand-raising or early weaning becomes necessary. Krecek (1971) has found that the standard practice of weaning rats at twenty-one days of age influences later behavior because ADH (antidiuretic hormone) activity is not fully mature until the animals are twenty-five or twenty-six days of age (which therefore might be the optimal time for weaning).

Marking for identification. The common practices of toe-clipping and ear-punching infant rodents for identification purposes have been found to alter maternal behavior in that the mother pays more attention to the marked pups, which in turn has been shown to influence their later behavior (Barnett and Burns, 1967). Various dyes may be applied to the skin of pups or to the hair of adults, but often these are groomed off within twenty-four hours. Cutting marks on the coat with clippers is a safe, innocuous method of marking individuals, provided all subjects receive an equal amount of handling. Subcutaneous injection of a nonabsorbable pigment such as India ink is a reliable way of marking subjects for long-term experiments. In general the trauma and change in social relationships as a consequence of ear-punching, toe-clipping, and tattooing constitute a variable which the experimenter should bear in mind.

Postsurgical care. Postsurgical care may influence a number of experiments. For example, "sham-operated" controls may receive less handling and tender loving care from laboratory personnel than the operated subjects, which may be taken home, exposed to an enriched environment, and so on. Such treatment could alter the significance of, say, the effects of early brain lesions on later behavior where the controls are kept under standard laboratory conditions while the lesion subjects receive very different care. In addition, the effects of returning an animal to its social group rather than to a separate cage to which it has been previously conditioned may influence recovery and possibly the experiment itself. The individual that is returned to its group may encounter a change in social relationships that results in fighting, subordination, or exclusion of the individual from the social group, any of which could be detrimental to the experiment. On the other hand, young animals, especially primates, may suffer separation depression when deprived of their mothers after surgery. It is surprising how well infant primates do when they are returned to their mothers after surgery. The infants can be returned as soon as they have recovered from anesthesia, which is very rapid when suitable anesthetic agents and antagonists are used.

EFFECTS OF ENVIRONMENTAL CHANGE

The importance of experience in a particular environment is related to the animal's ability to adapt to a new environment. The narrower the animal's range of experience, the more limited is its ability to adapt to more varied or different conditions. Each environmental change—for instance, from the rearing kennels to the laboratory animal facility to the animal research unit—entails some degree of adaptation. Adaptation is more protracted and psychophysiological stress is more pronounced where there is greater dissonance between consecutive environmental conditions. If the qualitative and quantitative complexity of consecutive environmental conditions is increased gradually, however, the adverse effects can be reduced (Fox, 1972a), although some time must be allowed at each step to enable the subject to adapt to the new conditions.

The period of adaptation to new surroundings and possibly to a new social hierarchy (if the animals are housed in groups) varies, depending on the individual's behavior phenotype and previous experiences, and may be prolonged in animals derived from random sources or from the wild. Recently captured monkeys may take as long as twelve months to adapt to the restricted environment of the animal facility and to develop a degree of physiological stability. In this respect there is clearly some advantage in using animals which have been "raised for the laboratory" under relatively impoverished cage conditions.

The combined emotional and physical stresses as a result of transportation, quarantine, worming, vaccination, and adaptation increase the susceptibility of the animals to disease, and it has been shown experimentally by Kurtsin (1968) that even wound healing may be protracted. Experimental procedures such as drug assays or surgery should clearly not be undertaken until the subjects have adapted or equilibrated psychophysiologically. In many animal facilities dogs are held for a minimum of four weeks to allow recovery from these stresses before they are considered suitable for most experimental procedures.

A number of specific problems can arise in laboratory animals as a result of deprivation of social and environmental stimuli (Fox, 1968). A rapid decline in weight may be indicative of nervous anorexia. After a period of time the animal may become withdrawn and asocial, may develop stereotyped activities or abnormal patterns of behavior such as aggressiveness, polydipsia, or polyphagia, or may indulge in excessive grooming or even automutilation. Coprophagia is a common vice in confined dogs and is extremely difficult to inhibit, although cages with slatted or wire floors will reduce the problem. Appreciation of the causes of these disturbances will greatly facilitate the choice of the most appropriate solution from the following alternatives: (1) discard the subject and select a more suitable one; (2) allow the animal to exercise outside the cage for short periods; (3) handle the animal and provide it with social contact with its own kind; (4) allow the animal visual access to companions in neighboring cages and feed it by hand.

Our observations about the effect of environmental and social factors on laboratory animals point to the need for a standard environmental "genotype" of laboratory animal care, just as a strain or a breed is selected and genetically standardized in order to reduce phenotype variability. One of the most important factors in the establishment of standardized animal care is rigorous programming of rearing and maintenance practices, handling, socialization, and environmental complexity. If standardized practices were adhered to by all research institutions, different genotype-environment interactions could be avoided and the production of animals of the same strain with phenotypes that differ widely from one institution to the next could be eliminated.

CHAPTER 5

ANIMAL FEELINGS AND FEELING FOR ANIMALS: HEALING THE BOND

Millions of people enjoy the company of animals because they give so much pleasure, expressing affection, playfulness, concern, interest, joyful greeting, and grateful satisfaction. These and other emotive behaviors we do not imagine. They are as real as the feelings they evoke in us. The subjective state or feelings of humans, cats, dogs, and other sentient beings when expressing various emotions must be similar, since they evoke similar affective responses.

The gulf that separates us from other animals is not our intelligence but our disbelief: our inability to accept their similar sentience and their emotional affinity with us. We should not demean their affinity as pathological dependence, or as the subversion of unconscious instincts by domestication to the extent that adult cats regard their "owners" simply as parent-providers and that dogs would sooner be with other dogs but are bonded to their "masters" as substitute pack leaders.

As our understanding of the ethos of cats, dogs, and other creatures wild and tame deepens, so must our understanding of the human-animal bond and of peoples' attitudes toward animals in various cultures, as well as psychohistorically. Otherwise our knowledge will be incomplete, and we will fail to fully comprehend much beyond self-serving utilitarian horizons. The "objective" language of the psychobiological sciences is not much help, tending to limit our horizons with mechanistic terminology. It is recognized more widely now that animals often display behavior patterns that communicate to us, empathetically and via their emotion-evoking distress calls, expressions and postures, a whole range of subjective states, such as separation anxiety, despair, grief, terror, as well as relief, playful good humor, satisfaction, concern, and even empathy, compassion, and altruism. But the semanticists of scientism have no objective synonyms for these subjective states. And so it is considered unscientific to allude to such states, but in truth we have no other words that do not sound anthropomorphic. Alternative, mechano-morphic terms like approach, avoidance, satiation, and consummation are unacceptably simplistic and give no intimation as to emotional or motivational state.

Some of these very human emotions I felt and witnessed in a Kashmir, India, village some years ago, when I saw a male pariah dog licking the sores and snapping at the flies around his mate's infected face. Both were emaciated, and he let the old bitch feed before him after I had thrown them some food. Such empathy and altruistic behavior are common to many animal species, not only to the human species. This ethologically documented evidence of deliberate care-giving behavior to others that are not simply immature offspring, is proof of a highly developed empathic sensibility in animals. Some investigators have claimed such sensibility, albeit rudimentary, in trees and other plants, as well as in insects, and other in-

Animal Feelings and Feeling for Animals

vertebrate and protoplasmic life forms. Be that as it may, when we begin to appreciate the significance of the sentient nature of other animals and of the universe itself,[1] our attitude toward and treatment of animals changes radically toward what might best be termed panempathic communion.

But when we do not live close to animals in their natural environs and see them only in the altered states of domestication and captive confinement, we can become alienated and unfamiliar with their ways, their ethos. So we deny them feelings, awareness, even sentience as well as intelligence, and in the process of denial we mechano-morphize them, seeing and even treating them as unfeeling machines. Or, we anthropomorphize them, unable to see them as they really are through the perceptual filters of sentimentality and objectification.

People who really see animals for the first time as fellow sentient beings become humane because they experience in other animals the kinship of sentience. This is not some deluded anthropomorphic projection, but a fact of rational human experience and responsiveness and the consequence of feral vision. I recall reading of the complete change in attitude of an Australian government dingo exterminator, who was hiding in the bush near a spring where tracks indicated that dingos came to drink at dusk. His task was to shoot whatever wild dogs came. A pair came to drink, and he killed one, who was slower and seemed to be led by its mate to the water hole. The government agent was shocked to find that the dingo he had shot was blind, had been blind for a long time, and was in excellent physical condition. Without the empathy and concern of his mate, this old blind dingo would have long perished. Realizing how caring dingos can be for each other in the Outback, the man never killed another dingo from that day on.

Concepts in Ethology

There are instances of wild animals seeking human assistance, like a bobcat that crawled out from cover to lie across a cross-country skier's skis and allow itself to be wrapped in a jacket and taken to a veterinary hospital to have festering porcupine quills removed. And what of the behavior of a rehabilitated orphan bobcat who brought her cubs, born in the wild, back to show the woman who had rescued and healed her?

There are also accounts of dogs who had been treated at a veterinary hospital, taking an injured stray animal back to the same hospital for treatment. These and other eye opening anecdotes reveal a degree of intelligence or sapience as well as sentience in animals that makes us wonder and challenge those attitudes that lead us to treat them without regard for their true natures. They move us to establish a new covenant of compassion with the entire sentient world. And until we are so moved and our empathy and feral vision close the distance between us and fellow creatures, the possibility of a truly humane society will forever elude us. We will also fall short of realizing our full human potential to be humane. Humane, like compassion, is neither a noun nor an adjective. It is a verb. To be humane means treating all living beings—human, plant, and animal—with compassion and reverential respect, including their environments and communities. It is not simply a name for animal welfare or protection, but a state of being in awareness that is the hallmark of a truly civilized society.

Healing Animals, Animal Healing

I quickly learned as a veterinary student some 35 years ago, working on various farms and seeing practice with large and small animal and zoo animal veterinary specialists, that many of the health and welfare problems of animals were caused by

Animal Feelings and Feeling for Animals

how they were treated; by how they had been selectively bred to have various desired traits and acquired genetic abnormalities; by how they had been raised; by the kind of environment and relationships they had during early development with their own kind and with their human caretakers; and by what kind and quality of food and living conditions they were provided to satisfy their basic physical and psychological needs during the rest of their lives.

I came to realize that the healing of animals and their well-being entailed healing the human-animal bond. This bond was in urgent need of repair because so much of the sickness and suffering of animals was due to how people perceived them and treated them. It also dawned on me that if people were not in a right, ethical, and equitable relationship (or in their right minds, so to speak), with fellow creatures, then the same probably held true for their relationships with their own kind and with the environment. So the key to preventing much human suffering and sickness was probably the same as for animals: the key was one of relationship and mindfulness; of compassion and empathy; of understanding and loving kindness.

This realization was hammered home many times when I visited various university laboratory animal research facilities and saw the small cages and pens in which cats, dogs, rhesus monkeys, and other creatures were incarcerated. What shocked me was seeing arboreal and highly social primates being housed for years alone in metal cages 3′ × 4′; and cats and dogs, who were formerly family pets, being kept in impoverished environments in which they were clearly disoriented, deprived, and distressed.

I investigated and reported[2] how these seriously inadequate conditions for laboratory animals created sick, stressed, and abnormal animals, making them dubious subjects for scientific study. Research findings from these animals had little medical relevance except perhaps to other creatures kept under comparable intolerable conditions.

While I saw—as a veterinarian and biomedical scientist—the status quo of laboratory animal care and use as being ethically and scientifically untenable, most of the United States biomedical research establishment rejected my findings and continued to defend all vivisection unconditionally.

The biomedical research industry has so much political and public influence that it can change truth and revise history. With a few phone calls and threatening letters, they demonstrated this power by making *Encyclopaedia Britannica* alter, in subsequent editions, my contribution to the 1991 revised edition, deleting all my reference to examples of cruel experimentation and to animal rights in subsequent editions to the *Dog* entry.

I have also experienced the lies, denial, ridicule, and concerted opposition of the agribusiness establishment that wants the status quo of intensive industrialized animal agriculture—so-called factory farming—to be maintained to further the economic interests of a powerful few. The many hidden costs are neither revealed to the public nor to shareholders. These include farm animal sickness and suffering; ecological damage; loss of nonrenewable natural resources from top soil to fossil fuels; loss of family farms; and the socio-economic demise of rural communities and once-sustainable agricultural practices. The role of animal-based agriculture in contributing to increased consumer diet- and food-safety-related health problems is also denied.

I have visited factory farms and feedlots and documented[3,4] how livestock and poultry are raised for human profit and consumption. Having seen alternative, more natural or ecological farming systems in the United States and in many other countries, I do not accept food (and fur) animal factories as

Animal Feelings and Feeling for Animals

normal and progressive "state of the art." I regard them as pathogenic environments for the animals, and *as being symptomatic of a seriously defective human-animal bond*. To develop and accept livestock and poultry production systems that entail treating animals as mere production units and that deny them their basic rights and behavioral needs, is surely indicative of an aberrant mutation in human consciousness; an attitude or state of mind that lacks empathetic sensibility. It is ethically blind because it has no vestige of feral vision.

While this mutation is such that we are neither in our right minds nor in right relationship with animals and Nature, it does not mean that we cannot change our minds and behavior. We can recover our feral vision to establish a more equitable relationship with animals and Nature—one based more on compassion, symbiosis and service, than on domination and exploitation. Then the possibility of building a global, humane, and sustainable society may be realized, but not until the liberation of animals from human bondage is seen as a spiritual and ethical imperative linked with our own survival and well-being.

The human-animal bond is as ancient as our earliest ancestors emerging from the dawn of time. Animals were the referentials that helped us define what it means to be human and what it means to be Other.

As Professor Calvin Schwabe has shown in his seminal book *Cattle Priests and Progress in Medicine*[5], the first veterinarians were also priests and healers of people. This noble tradition of the veterinarian as a latter-day shaman, or interlocutor, between humankind and the animal kingdom is best expressed when we begin to examine the human-animal bond and seek to correct it wherever and whenever the basic bioethical principle of *ahimsa*, of avoiding harm or injury to an animal, is violated.

Concepts in Ethology

Animals have served us in myriad ways over millennia and we owe them a great debt of gratitude. This gratitude we have yet to fully express in a more compassionate, egalitarian, and mutually enhancing symbiosis, since this bond today is primarily one of domination and exploitation rather than of service and communion.

Scientific research is rediscovering the many human benefits of a strong human-animal bond, or what I prefer to call the human-nonhuman animal bond, since we humans are animals after all. As other animals have been shown in a variety of documented studies[6] to help people overcome great emotional difficulties and physical and psychological handicaps, so we can help them, by saving endangered species, by restoring and protecting their habitats, and by alleviating the suffering of animals through the art and science of veterinary medicine.

Humaneness Pays

Several studies have revealed how a positive, affectionate social bond with animals helps enhance disease resistance in laboratory animals, the productivity of farm animals, and the trainability of dogs and other species.

It has now been scientifically documented that when animal caretakers express a negative attitude toward farm animals, and when the animals under their care are afraid of humans, then such animals are under a chronic state of stress. This stress has been shown to reduce the numbers of offspring that sows produce, the numbers of eggs laying hens produce, and the amount of milk dairy cows give. Meat quality and growth rates in broilers, piglets, and beef calves may also be adversely affected. In contrast, where farmers, farmhands, ranchers, and cowboys treat animals gently and with understanding so as not

Animal Feelings and Feeling for Animals

to trigger fear reactions and induce a chronic state of stress, and especially when there is a strong social bond between caretaker and animal, the animals are healthier, more productive, and profitable. In sum, humaneness pays.[7]

But this evident fact may be discounted in favor of the cost-savings of developing large-scale, labor-saving, intensive livestock and poultry systems where one person is in charge of hundreds, even thousands of animals. Such labor-saving "efficiencies" have been criticized for decades by those who believe that farm animals need individual attention or at least regular daily inspection. It may be argued that a good stockperson with a positive attitude toward animals on a large factory farm will do a better job than one who is indifferent or whom the animals fear. However, working in large, intensive production systems has been shown to adversely affect the behavior and attitudes of stockpersons, notably, causing increased aggressive behavior, which has a detrimental effect on the animals' welfare and productivity.[8]

There is a distinction between humanely directing an animal's telos (final end or ecological purpose) for one's own benefit, and disregarding both telos and ethos (or intrinsic nature) and manipulating both, as in factory farming and genetic engineering, for exclusively human benefit. The good farmer and pastoralist knew how best to profit from the telos of plants and animals without harming either their ethos or the ecos—the ecosystem—as a creative participant or symbiote (Figure 23). This distinction between kindly use and selfish exploitation is the difference between sustainable and non-sustainable living. The difference between treating animals and other life forms as ends in themselves, respecting their ethos and ecological role, and of using them as a means to satisfy purely human ends is a central issue of bioethics.

Concepts in Ethology

ETHOS
(nature of animals)

TELOS
(ultimate purpose)

ECOS
(nature of ecosystems)

FIG. 23. A Venn diagram illustrating the dynamic interplay and interdependence of an animal's ethos, telos, and ecos that together help ensure the animal's overall well-being.

The consequences of this latter utilitarian attitude and relationship are potentially harmful economically, environmentally, socially, and spiritually. The essence of right livelihood is surely to accommodate the interests and intrinsic value of other members of the biotic community and to enable those species whom we have domesticated—as well as ourselves—to live according to their natures, where ethos, telos, and ecos are fully integrated and harmoniously actualized.

Animal Feelings and Feeling for Animals

The keeping of wild animals in captivity for public entertainment, the selective breeding of genetically defective "bonsai" pets, and the genetic engineering of animals for various commercial purposes also illustrate how one-sided the human-animal bond has become.[9]

In sum, natural living, like natural or organic farming, has its own integrity. Ironically, in the process of "denaturing" animals under the dehumanizing yolk of industrial-scale domestication, we do no less to ourselves and suffer the consequences under the guise of "civilized" necessity and progress. But there is nothing civilized or progressive in this utilitarian attitude toward life since it ultimately reduces the value of human life and all life to sheer utility, which is the nihilistic telos of technocratic imperialism and materialistic determinism.

Until we fully address and repair the human-nonhuman animal bond *and this is, I believe, the primary task of veterinarians and humanitarians,* the world will continue to suffer the adverse consequences of a pathological human attitude toward fellow creatures and Nature.

A healthy, or relatively healthy, bond between urban people and their "pets" or animal companions, will not suffice. Our bond with each other and with all living beings will be restored when the bioethic of reverential respect for the sanctity of life is universal: And when there is understanding of the threefold nature of every being and all becoming—ethos, telos, and ecos—the interdependent unity of which must be protected, nurtured, and celebrated. It is enlightened self-interest to preserve this unity as best we can in the course of satisfying our basic needs. This is because a society that destroys Nature's biodiversity and resources will become materially bankrupt. Similarly, we will become spiritually bankrupt if there is no collective regard for the intrinsic value and ethos of animals, and of their telos or purpose in the ecological community. It is this Earth community, not simply the human community, that we must all come to serve if we are to survive, prosper, and evolve.

Postscript: Animal Rights and Human Liberation

Animals can't answer for themselves, so who is to speak for them? Those who speak for them, using legalistic rights language, will never get very far because such language is locked within the mind-set of Greek (Aristotelian) rationalism and Cartesian dualism[1]. Their opponents reason that animal rights are subordinate to human rights and interests, because they believe humans are superior. Furthermore, the question of animal rights is judged from a point of reference that is derived from Roman law and jurisprudence. Thus the violation of animals' rights is acceptable if it benefits the empire or society in any way.

This Graeco-Roman rationalism found fertile soil in Judaism and Christianity arguably because of their anthromorphic conception of divinity and consequential anthropocentric and chauvinistic world view, and because the leaders of these faith-traditions were human and therefore fallible and corruptible. It was never beneath most priests to slaughter and eat the fatted calf, to invest in livestock, or for their orders to invest in real estate, or in war, and today to speculate in the stock market.

Consequently, the voice of these monotheistic religious traditions has been almost silent in speaking out on behalf of animal rights. This was not, I believe, to avoid the Aristotelian trap that is set to rationalize human superiority over all creatures and Creation, but to actually preserve the status quo of animal utility and human superiority.

In order for animal rights to prevail and be accepted by all, it must come from an ethical basis that is spiritual rather

Animal Feelings and Feeling for Animals

than legalistic or moralistic. It must come from the heart of compassion and from reason that informs that we and all creatures are related, part of the same divine creation and conception. Otherwise, the necessary spiritual transformation of humanity will not be accomplished by those who seek to defend animals and protect them from our inhumanity. From this perspective therefore, the spirituality of animal rights is a challenge to both organized religion and Western civilization. It is a call for a new religion, ethics, and social order.

The recovery of our humanity is a spiritual process, not one of law and order or rationalism and scientism. This is the ultimate task of all who still have empathy for animals and who are concerned about the fate of Earth's creation: The recovery of our humanity, compassion, humility, empathy, natural wisdom, and reverential respect for all Creation.

Our perception of the world—how we see other life forms, Nature's creations and "resources"—is influenced by how we value and feel for and about them. When we rid ourselves of all cultural programming and selfish wants and expectations, our perception changes. When we are loved by an animal, as when we love an animal, or a tree or some natural place, our perception changes. Too often that perceptual change is fleeting and we quickly return to our habitual ways of perception and of being and relating. We may or may not be aware of the splitting or separation that occurs when we shift from one way of seeing to another. The irony and ethical inconsistency may escape us—like the woman who loves her cats but wears a wild cat fur coat, and the biomedical research scientist who plays with his Golden Retriever before he goes to the laboratory to experiment on dogs. The ultimate irony for ethical vegetarians is that people say they love animals but eat them none the less.

Concepts in Ethology

Many rationalists, often with a science background, believe that life is not a process and expression of anything sacred or divine, but is a consequence of pure chance. Less thoughtful materialists or avowed atheists must deny or sublimate any feeling for the sacred, the *mysterium tremendum* that arises naturally from childhood's sense of awe and wonder. Parents, teachers, peers, and culture too often combine and conspire to crush this childhood gift of primordial feral perception. This way of seeing and being Walt Whitman described so eloquently in a child who became everything he beheld.

It is on the basis of this primordial feral vision that our sense of kinship with all life develops, along with the sense of self and the capacity to empathize. From empathy such human attributes as compassion and ethical sensibility arise naturally. When the development of feral vision is inhibited, the development of the whole person is impaired. Morality and law and order must be imposed from without when there is no internal, spontaneously arising empathic sensitivity, and ethical sensibility. In such a society, as we have today, feral vision leads to spiritual anarchy and the call to liberate all creatures and Creation from the inhumane and selfish dominion of those who see the world simply as a resource; as matter without spirit; as theirs by divine decree. The whole of Creation is not a means to human ends. Every being is an end unto itself. As Thomas Berry sees it, the universe is not a collection of objects but a communion of subjects.

From a purely anthropocentric perspective that sees Nature as a resource and that has no sense of kinship with animals, world peace, justice, and the integrity and future of Creation will never be secured. With feral vision the spiritual anarchist sees peace, justice, and the integrity and future of Creation from an anthropocosmic perspective. This more

Animal Feelings and Feeling for Animals

holistic mind-set entails a paradigm shift from the conventional, human-centered world view. It is a difficult shift to achieve when the primordial feral perception of childhood has not been nurtured and has instead been inhibited and allowed to atrophy.

The recovery of feral vision is linked ultimately with the recovery of our humanity. Sometimes this vision is restored by great personal tragedy, by near-fatal illness, a near-death experience or by the devotion of an animal. There are religious and spiritual traditions, some old and some new, like the vision quest that can help us regain this way of seeing and of being. Those who lack such vision cannot know what they are not seeing and feeling until they have gone through the paradigm shift. Only then can they look back on who and what they where before their vision was restored.

How is this shift in consciousness and perception achieved? As prevention is the best medicine, it is best to nurture the primordial feral vision in childhood via humane and environmental education and spiritual guidance to facilitate the development of empathy and ethical sensibility. But when we have an entire industrial civilization based on the values of materialism and consumerism, and economic and political forces that maintain the status quo and collective mind-set, then the possibility of a *metanoia,* a radical change in consciousness and perception, seems infinitely remote. It is until those with feral vision, the spiritual anarchists of this age, begin to challenge the status quo and show, for instance, that the economy is as nonsustainable as it is socially unjust. In the process, they will help empower consumers with an alternative vision that enables them to see that the corruption of politicians is merely a reflection of the corruption of the spirit of contemporary society. Like the child in Hans Christian Andersen's story who proclaimed that the Emperor was not wearing any clothes, so a populace, with feral vision, can see the sham and artifice of those who seek power and profit at the expense of their own kind, of animal kind, and of Earth's creation.

In Nature's image and living presence still, we have our being and becoming. In God's image, Nature—and every sentient being and natural form, process, and phenomenon, from the atoms of matter to the genes of life—is a reflection thereof.

The spiritual world view is normative for those who have not lost their feral vision. Little wonder such people feel alienated from the consensus reality their peers and elders embrace; the reality that condones the commoditization of all life and sees nothing sacred or of significance beyond the values and aspirations of a purely materialistic, consumptive existence. When those with feral vision make their vision and concerns known, but rarely understood, they are too often ostracized and ridiculed as being unrealistic, idealistic, anti-establishment. In past ages they were variously shunned, excommunicated, persecuted, and even burned at the stake.

It is inconceivable for those who defend the status quo of inhumanity to accept that this status quo is the very cause of all our worldly tribulations and sufferings. And that, on the grounds of reason and compassion, any rational being would take every step to change this status quo: The status quo that speaks of rights but denies them; that speaks of justice but is unjust; that speaks of morality but has no life-ethic that is not self-centered; and that has no values higher than materialism, nor horizon beyond the acquisition of wealth and power. This "system" cannot change itself. We created it, and so did our forefathers. So we must change it. With feral vision and the spiritual anarchy that arises therefrom, as more people of all ages "go wild" and reclaim their humanity, their authenticity

Animal Feelings and Feeling for Animals

and significance in life, this gentle revolution—and the evolution of our species—will begin.

It is beginning now, this change in perception, in our consciousness and how we relate to and value other sentient beings and the living Earth. Thomas Berry (personal communication) captures this self-transformative process through his own feral vision in the following words:

> The primordial awakening of the soul is among the most exquisite moments in the story of the universe, surely of the planet Earth. To see the stars in the night sky, to hear the mockingbird in the early dawn, to taste the water from a hillside spring—such experiences drench us in wonder. Life is experienced as fulfillment. The universe and the human soul were made exactly for each other. Any effort to diminish their intimacy with each other can only lead to disaster.

So in conclusion, the animals, the trees, the Earth, and all living things do speak for themselves when we listen and pay attention. I would not ask anyone "Are you for or against animal rights?" but rather "Are you for or against peace, justice, compassion, and the integrity and future of Creation?"

Our species is now at a biological and evolutionary crossroads. As Teilhard de Chardin observed some 30 years ago in his book *The Future of Man,* we have reached the point in our biological evolution where we have one final choice to make. That is between suicide and adoration. When the world economy, and the politics, policies, and priorities of nation-states cease to operate in an ethical vacuum totally devoid of reverential respect for all life, then we will be more secure. Only that which is sacred is secure. And from the hindsight of feral vision we see that reverential respect for all life is enlightened self-interest. It is the highest value to live by and the only one worth dying for. In our recognition and acceptance of animal rights, not as some legal or moral principle, but as a spiritual and ethical imperative, we will realize our own liberation in the process.

Concepts in Ethology

Animals on the Global Agenda of Human Concern and Responsibility

The rights of Nature, humans, and animals are interconnected and interdependent. Animals fulfill many important roles in society. They are thus worthy of our respect and humane treatment. Their health and welfare are inseparable from the health and well-being of society. Animal cruelty and suffering should be prevented in all countries for the moral and ethical integrity and future of society. Wild animals fulfill many vital roles in natural ecosystems. The health and welfare of wild animals are inseparable for the vitality and well-being of Nature. Animals' place in Nature should therefore be respected for the ecological integrity and future of Nature. Caring for creatures and Creation is the key to a humane and sustainable economy and global community.

Notes

1. For an informative and inspiring description of this evolving process, see *The Universe Story* by Brian Swimme and Thomas Berry (1994). San Francisco, CA: Harper.

2. M. W. Fox (1986) *Laboratory Animal Husbandry, Ethology Welfare and Experimental Variables.* Albany, NY: State University of New York Press.

3. M. W. Fox (1984) *Farm Animals: Husbandry, Behavior and Veterinary Practice.* Baltimore, MD: University Park Press.

4. M. W. Fox (1986) *Agricide: The Hidden Crisis That Affects Us All.* New York: Schocken Books.

5. (1978) Minneapolis, MN: University of Minnesota Press.

6. For a recent comprehensive review, see A. T. B. Edney (1992) Companion animals and human health. *Veterinary Record,* April 4, p. 285–87.

7. For a comprehensive review of this fascinating and important aspect of the human-animal bond, see P. H. Hemsworth, et al. (1993) The human-animal relationship in agriculture and its consequences for the animal. *Animal Welfare (Universities Federation for Animal Welfare)* 2:33–51.

Animal Feelings and Feeling for Animals

8. For details, see M. F. Seabrook (1994) The effect of production systems on the behavior and attitudes of stockpersons. pp. 252–8 in Proc. 4th Zodiac Symposium. *Biological Basis of Sustainable Animal Production.* EAAP. Publ. No. 67. Waneningen, The Netherlands.

9. For documentation of these and other ethically questionable forms of animal exploitation, see:

M. W. Fox (1990) *Inhumane Society: The American Way of Exploiting Animals.* New York, NY: St. Martin's Press.

M. W. Fox (1992) *Superpigs and Wondercorn: The Brave New World of Biotechnology and Where It May All Lead.* New York: Lyons and Burford.

CHAPTER 6

THE BIOETHICS OF ANIMAL AND ENVIRONMENTAL PROTECTION

From Ethology to Ethics

Comparative studies in anatomy, physiology, and pathology in various animal species can enhance our understanding of human evolution, adaptation, and response to stress and pathogens. Likewise, comparative studies in ethology, behavioral development, and pathology in animals can further our understanding of the biology and pathology of human behavior, development, and social pathology.

As ethologists' attitudes toward animals have changed in recent years, so have their concepts and the kinds of questions and hypotheses they have elaborated about animals' behavior and awareness. For example, Frans de Waal has traced the origins of empathy, altruism, and the evolution of morality in nonhuman animals.[1] Aside from the fact that humans are not the only beings on Earth endowed with these "higher" attributes,

Bioethics of Animal and Environmental Protection

comparative studies of human and nonhuman behavior help give us insights about our own nature, especially with regard to the natural selection of those innate, genetically transmitted capacities for human aggression and selfishness, altruism, and compassion. We humans, like de Waal's studies of our closest primate relatives, are chimeric beings with the innate potentialities for both good and evil.

The dark side of human nature—our capacity to do evil—is what Van Rensselaer Potter calls our "fatal flaw."[2] Potter describes this flaw, which is genetically programmed and no doubt helped us survive eons ago, as "the tendency to emphasize the here and now and not to worry about the long-term future." He sees this flaw as a major limiting factor in the blossoming of global bioethics. It is the desire for immediate gratification, epitomized by consumerism. He contends that, "The fatal flaw is probably in all of us in our 'animal' genes, but is countered by a set of 'ethical' genes that moderate the 'flaw' with a concern for future survival. . . . "

Parents, teachers, and social reformers should be alert to its manifestation in children and help educate children to understand and therefore gain better self-control of this dark side. In the process, their empathic and ethical sensibilities will be awakened and directed toward bioethical awareness and behavior. If Frans de Waal's apes and monkeys can do this with their offspring, then surely we can do it with ours.

In the human species, morality and ethics, or a lack thereof, have profound consequences. No study of human behavior and of human-human- and human-nonhuman relationships can ignore the influence of moral codes and ethics in how humans relate to each other and value and treat other animals. In essence, ethology leads inevitably to the study of the biological (genetic), acquired, cultural or ideological bases of ethical decision making processes, moral sensibility, and such traits as empathy and altruism. These traits are not exclusively human, and they clearly play a vital role in the adaptive success and continuation of a variety of mammalian species. This underscores the need for we humans to realize that ethical behavior has more to do with our own survival and success than with some qualitative virtue that has no practical relevance in a world of competitive individualism where only the "fittest" (the most aggressive and powerful) survive.

Bioethics, Behavior, and Conflicting Values

The basic intention of bioethics, therefore, is to foster those values and principles that are best for the continuation of life on Earth; and help minimize any harm that we may cause to other beings, human and nonhuman. Bioethics can help us maximize the fruits of human creativity for the benefit of all life without harming the integrity of Creation or violating the sanctity of life.

The battle of conflicting human values or world views today is not simply between the Creationists and Evolutionists, or between religious faith and scientific rationalism. It is fundamentally between the polarities of human nature with its affinities for good and evil, and between those who see life as more than matter and others who believe that only matter matters. This dialectic between the naturalists or vitalists and the mechanists or materialists cannot be reconciled by science or religion alone. Rather, a synthesis of scientific knowledge, especially of biology and of the spirituality of religious traditions that translate into ethical principles, may help in this reconciliation. Bioethics is precisely that synthesis of bioscience and ethical principles that can help guide and constrain human behavior for the good of all.

We may, as a species, have progressed in the realms of scientific discovery and technological ingenuity, but in the realm

Bioethics of Animal and Environmental Protection

of bioethics, we have been at a standstill for centuries, if not millennia. This is because we have not effectively addressed the question of our responsibilities toward animals and nature. We have set arbitrary legal limits and regulations, and voluntary codes and guidelines concerning our use of animals, but we have failed to resolve a central issue of concern to many. That issue is the propriety of exploiting animals for any purpose that entails their suffering, deprivation of a natural existence and/or death; and our unquestioned presumption that to do so is right and proper if it is for the benefit of society.

Existing animal protection laws are as inconsistent internationally as they are within nations and regions. Some species have less protection than others and some forms of animal exploitation are above the law. For example, poultry in the United States are excluded from any protection under the Animal Welfare and Humane Slaughter Acts, and animals destined for human consumption are raised and treated in ways that would be criminal violations of state anticruelty laws if they were dogs instead of pigs or calves.

These ethical and legal inconsistencies in animal protection and how people behave toward animals are rooted in a long history of religious and cultural traditions and values. But they are being subject to more rigorous scrutiny as different cultures are being drawn together by two forces: concerns over loss of species, of biodiversity and wildlife habitat (including marine ecosystems); and conventions and agreements currently being made with respect to world trade. Emerging points of concern and contention include how different countries protect endangered species, the environment, and natural resources. How they treat domestic animals, principally those that are raised, transported, and killed for human consumption, and what drugs they have been given, like growth promotants and antibiotics.

Concepts in Ethology

If there is a common ground for these different countries, it is the unquestioned acceptance of exploiting animals for commercial purposes. Yet this acceptance is based upon an unexamined, a priori assumption that such exploitation is ethical. This assumption is based on the belief by those who profit from exploiting animals that there is nothing morally wrong in regarding animal life as a means to satisfy human ends. This belief is shared by all cultures that have a common history of exploiting animals. This long history of human exploitation of animals over millennia has set an unquestioned precedent for its continuation as a socially condoned behavioral and attitudinal norm.

As the human population has exploded, along with a proliferation of wants and needs, so has the extent and intensity of animal exploitation, from fishing, hunting, and trapping to raising more and more animals intensively for food, fur, and fibre, and using more in biomedical research and product safety tests. Furthermore, wildlife habitat is being polluted and destroyed at an accelerating rate.

A comparative ethological evaluation of the behavior and ecological fitness of wolves and deer, lynx and Arctic hares, and of humans and their livestock, reveal many parallels and inversions. These carnivores take meat as a dietary staple, and so do we humans. Wolves and lynx show us that all meat-eating species in natural ecosystems are *very few* in number. But the human species population will soon be six billion. Rather than change its behavior and no longer regard and consume meat as a dietary staple, an unnatural, highly destructive and toxic agriecosystem has been developed to fatten billions of livestock. Their ecological role is not utilized since more and more are now being kept in factories and feedlots.

Bioethics of Animal and Environmental Protection

Farm Animal Ethology and Bioethics

It concerns me that intensively raised, "factory" farmed animals are kept under conditions that cause stress and distress, because the nature or *ethos* of these animals is of little or no significance in industrial agrisystems. Furthermore, their *telos* or ecological purpose is not utilized as it is in organic, ecological, and sustainable agriculture. These animals are denied even a semblance of a natural environment or *ecos*. Their *ethos*, their instincts, wants and needs, are closely linked with their *telos* and *ecos* so as to fulfill their appropriate ecological role by contributing to the maintenance of the bioregional ecosystem (Figure 23). The *telos* of farm and other domestic and captive animals has been redirected to satisfy exclusively human ends. This is the essential point of imbalance in the "human-animal bond." It must be more reciprocal and mutually enhancing so that farm animals are able to reassume their natural ecological roles. This would automatically result in the *ethos* and thus the overall well-being of these animals being more fully realized. The essential bioethical criterion of humane animal husbandry and optimal welfare standards is therefore based upon providing animals with the right kinds of environments that satisfy their basic ethological requirements.

An egalitarian bioethical principle, derived from the anthropocentric concept of justice, that recognizes the interdependence of humans, animals, and the environment, I would call the principle of *symbiotic harmony*. This principle seeks to promote and maintain mutually enhancing symbiotic relationships between humans, animals, and the environment. It combines utilitarianism with compassion and reverential respect for the life community. Symbiotic harmony is dependent, therefore, on environmental protection, eco-justice, respect for

Concepts in Ethology

the rights and interests of animals wild and domestic, and social justice.

With compassion as its compass, the all encompassing circle of bioethics enables us to give equal and fair consideration to animal, environmental, and social concerns. Bioethics thus helps reconcile the polemics of animal versus human rights, and of conservation versus exploitation of natural resources. Andrew Fraser was one of the first veterinarians to recognize the importance of bioethics in improving animal welfare, defining animal bioethics as "a constitution of integrated ethical practices and of animal welfare principles, in mankind's use of sentient animals, serving to control suffering." He sees the speciality of bioethics as "the pursuit, application, and maintenance of human principles in the care and husbandry of sentient animals, in the interest of their well-being."[3]

When the public is led to believe that their well-being and freedom from disease is dependent upon the continued use of animals in biomedical research and that there are no alternatives, then the utilitarian argument in favor of vivisection receives the unwarranted support of a misinformed public. From the perspectives of alternative medical paradigms very different from the conventional Western allopathic one like those of alternative, holistic, Ayruvedic, and Taoist medicine, the suffering and killing of animals to find cures for human diseases is scientifically invalid, medically irrelevant, and thus unethical.

We must reflect on this often quoted statement by Albert Schweitzer from his book *Philosophy of Civilization* that encapsulates his opinion on animal research as follows: "Wherever any animal is forced into the service of man the sufferings which it has to bear on that account are the concern of everyone of us. No one ought to permit, in so far as we can prevent it, pain or suffering for which he will not take that responsibility."[4] The responsibility to make every effort to prevent animal suffering, as by the adoption of alternatives to experimenting on animals, is surely an ethical imperative. From a non-anthropocentric perspective, deliberately causing animals to suffer for any reason is unethical behavior.

Since animals, like we humans, are members of the life community, they should be treated as subjects of moral concern. The notion that animals are not worthy of moral consideration because they are amoral and cannot establish a morality-based contractual agreement with us is one of the absurd products of over 2,000 years of anthropocentrism since the time of Aristotle and the Greek Epicureans and Stoics. We should give animals moral consideration in the name of compassion precisely because we are human, rather than deny them because they are not human.

What must end is our continuing to behave in an ethical vacuum and to unquestioningly accept all forms of animal and nature exploitation, for reasons of custom, convenience, and commerce, that cause animals to suffer or have harmful environmental consequences. Every society that accepts the suffering of animals in the name of profit and convenience loses its compassion. How long can any human association survive and prosper without compassion? Compassion is the boundless and only absolute ethic within the human realm that qualifies us to be human and which is the foundation of a truly humane and sustainable society.

Notes

1. F. de Waal (1996) *Good Natured: The Origins of Right and Wrong in Humans and Other Animals.* Cambridge, MA: Harvard University Press.
2. V. R. Potter (1995) Global bioethics: linking genes to ethical behavior. *Perspectives in Biol. and Med.* 39:118–31.

3. See A. F. Fraser (1992) The History of Applied Ethology in *Animal Welfare.* J. H. Seamer and F. W. Quimby (eds.). Proc. Animal Welfare Sessions XXIV World Veterinary Congress, Rio de Janiero Aug 1991. Animal Welfare Committee of the World Veterinary Association. London p. 14–25.

4. A. Schweitzer (1988) *Philosophy of Civilization.* Buffalo, NY: Prometheus Books.

CONCLUSIONS

In this monograph several inferences and insights into human behavior have been drawn from studies of animal behavior through analogy and homology. Comparative studies can and do provide us with a biological basis for understanding man, as exemplified by the holistic approach of the ethologist in studying social ecology and by the interdisciplinary approach of the developmental psychobiologist in defining critical and sensitive periods in ontogeny, but there is a limit to the value and application of animal studies. Although the studies reviewed in chapter 3, for example, provide valuable animal models of various developmental disorders in human beings, I believe that the relevance of many of these studies to child development and psychiatry is tenuous. When an investigator claims to have a primate model for maternal deprivation, we must be extremely cautious in applying his or her findings to humans because the interacting variables to which a growing child is exposed are far more complex than those to which primates in laboratories are exposed. If we wish to study development from a clinical viewpoint, we should focus our energies upon direct ethological and ontogenetic observations of human infants and not diffuse our resources in the development of animal models which can take us only so far.

Concepts in Ethology

Many of the models and concepts of ethology are, of course, relevant to clinical problems in both veterinary and human medicine. Ethological principles also have direct applicability to laboratory animal science and large animal (livestock) husbandry, where the quality of a research animal and the productivity of a farm animal, respectively, may be enhanced. In addition, a better understanding of the behavioral characteristics of animals may lead to improvements in their mental health and to more humane treatment of them generally by their owners and handlers. Nevertheless, many problems and phenomena are peculiar to man, and animal studies can help us relatively little in understanding these (except perhaps to show that they are unique to *Homo sapiens*).

Man is not simply a "naked ape" composed of instincts and animal desires. For example, man has a symbolic way of communicating and sharing concepts which we can use to recount or even to relive past events, to plan for the future, and to share predictions and expectations. Our ability to learn through observation or imitation, our innate curiosity, and our creative playfulness are capacities which enable us to acquire information culturally as well as genetically, to develop new skills, and to express new conceptual worlds in our ideas and in material ways. Whereas a bee constructs its hive by virtue of an innate blueprint, we can elaborate our own blueprints. Man's capacity for self-programming is no less innate than the bee's hive-building blueprint.

Some of the programming of the individual by his or her society, however, can result in conflict (Figure 24). Conflict and suffering can arise when the inner-directed, programmed needs are in opposition to other-directed programs. To an extent the contemporary consensus of one generation may serve to inhibit the growth potential of the next generation (individually or as a group) whereas ideally the established values should provide a

```
(Self-limiting)                    (Self-actualizing)
Power-control                         Awareness
     |                                    |
Status-success                     Creative freedom
     |                                    |
Recognition                            Love
     ↑                                    ↑
ACQUIRED (EGOIC) NEEDS          TRANSPERSONAL NEEDS
     ↑
     |          ⎧   Trust
     |          ⎪     |
Over-dependency ⎨   Belonging
Insecurity      ⎪     |
     ↑          ⎪   Acceptance
     |          ⎪     |
     |          ⎩   Companionship
     |                  ↑
     |          SOCIO-EMOTIONAL NEEDS
     |          ⎧    Sex
     |          ⎪     |
Privation       ⎪   Shelter
Repression     ⎨     |
Frustration     ⎪    Food
                ⎪     |
                ⎪   Water
                ⎪     |
                ⎩    Air
                      ↑
                PHYSICAL NEEDS
```

FIG. 24. Lack of fulfillment of basic physical needs in humans leads to privation, repression, and frustration. Social and emotional needs, if not met, may give rise to insecurity, "identity crisis," and dependency. (The self-limiting egocentric needs such as the need for power may compensate for frustration of social and emotional needs.) Western society generally reinforces the egoic needs more than the transpersonal needs.

stabilizing template and an orientation for continued growth and evolution. Certainly in the course of growing up, actualizing personal potentials, and maintaining a center of self in relation to others the individual must develop the ability to recognize needs that are in conflict and needs that are self-limiting. Conflict between the need to belong and the fear of rejection, the self-limiting egocentric pursuits of success and power, and the stress of maintaining status, for example, are common causes of emo-

Concepts in Ethology

tional suffering (both psychic and somatic). The need hierarchy developed by Maslow (1968), the founder of the humanistic psychology movement, is relevant to many of the social and intrapersonal ills of modern man. A shift in needs and values entails a shift in perception and cognition from egocentric dependency to a freer "being" awareness. The world is seen as it is rather than through a filter of projected needs and introjected hopes and fears. In some cases the aid of a good therapist is necessary to help us realize our capacity to "see" ourselves and to assume responsibility for ourselves, so that we may then continue to grow and to actualize our potentials (Figure 25).

FIG. 25. Hypothetical schema of the potential growth of human awareness. Development can continue exponentially throughout life; each turn in the spiral represents a higher level of awareness or complexity of consciousness. The dotted circle represents "maturity," a point at which the individual may become fixed ontologically in a particular role or value-determined conceptual space.

Conclusions

Man was originally a hunter and a gatherer who lived with others in small groups; this was the tribal stage during which the individual was bound in a complex familial web of kinship, shared rituals, and taboos. The total population increased rapidly when agriculture developed some ten thousand years ago, and the size of the groups grew with the rise of urban centers. With the expansion of complex technology during the last two hundred years, modern urban man often discovers that he no longer has the social support of a tribe or even an extended family. Our present situation involves adaptation to a new set of social and environmental factors to which the species as a whole has never before been exposed (Figure 26). The tribe's collective ego is replaced by individ-

FIG. 26. Schema of evolution of human consciousness and social organization. *1*. Tribal stage. *2*. Individual stage. *3*. Supratribal stage. The asterisks denote visionary teachers who lead human development toward stage 3. The arrows respectively indicate regression to stage 2 (because the individual fears a loss of identity upon approaching stage 3) or regression to stage 1 (because the individual seeks a feeling of "oneness with awareness" in the tribal or communal stage).

Concepts in Ethology

uality which, although giving freedom from social repressions, still carries the need for conformity but now to an anonymous community or to the consensus of nonrelatives. Even a sense of community is lacking in many suburban developments. Isolation, loneliness, and identity crisis underpin the "normal" neuroses and social pathologies of today, which are aggravated by the depersonalizing mechanization of man in corporate organizations. Many social needs (Figure 24) remain unfulfilled or are frustrated while a materialistic society tends to reward and reinforce the higher egocentric needs rather than the transpersonal, self-actualizing ones.

This era of pathological individualism (as an adaptation to depersonalization) and blind nationalism is the age of personal suffering and of international misunderstanding, conflict, and war. The most urgent priorities for research and action are clearly in the realm of human awareness, communication, and consciousness-raising directed toward improving human relationships, personal growth, and the mental health of the individual. Only then will humans care for each other and so begin to change the structure and values of society from within. Only then will we assume our full responsibility as the steward of the earth which today we pollute and overexploit. As I see it, the only alternative to acceptance of this responsibility is the destruction of the biosphere including humanity. Perhaps man's "original sin" was committed when we developed agriculture ten thousand years ago, but our contemporary sin is our ignorance (or our enculturated blindness to reality) and our failure to accept responsibility for the consequences of our own actions.

Ethnocentricity and egocentricity typify the state of the species as a whole at this stage. Ethnocentricity and cultural barriers are beginning to give way in the face of technoinvolution (economic interdependence, mass communication,

Conclusions

and so on), but the undermining or the destruction of the traditions and values of minority groups and of underdeveloped nations causes suffering to the individuals in these groups during the period of enculturation into a more global technosphere. Today's "lost generations" of North and South American Indians and of Eskimos, for example, are living proof of the many hardships that attend cultural dissolution when there has not been either an opportunity for gradual assimilation into the megaculture or freedom to choose to live alternative, traditional life-styles. The barriers of egocentricity are also being slowly broken down, as witnessed by the movement in the Western hemisphere to assess and develop individual human potential through encounter groups, body awareness training, ecopsychology and creation—centered spirituality.

The dissolution of ethnocentricity and egocentricity, possibly facilitated by technoinvolution, is leading to the third evolutionary stage of man (Figure 26) wherein a global "compressive socialization," to quote Teilhard de Chardin (1971), or a planetarization of consciousness, as described by Rudyar (1972), is possible. But many barriers which develop from within society stand in the way of this logical evolutionary step. The global socioeconomic and political involvement of the United States via the World Trade Organization is one example of such a cognitive barrier. Education in its broadest sense may help to open the doors of perception so that eventually the earth might be one world instead of a world of separate realities divided by ethnocentric and egocentric walls as it is today.

The concept of global brotherhood, a supratribal community, evokes skepticism in many. Perhaps they feel a pessimism about man's basic nature which, according to some, is

Concepts in Ethology

innately destructive. There is no evidence, however, of a basic drive in humans to destroy their fellows; although such a drive perhaps could be programmed into man's behavior by indoctrination or could be triggered by misunderstanding or national paranoia, it could also be programmed out or sublimated or redirected. Our specie's flexibility is our strength as well as our weakness.

Some may reject the notion of a supratribal community for fear of a loss of identity or of individuality and personal freedom. The global community would actually personalize rather than depersonalize, since it would be composed of open, trusting people with concern for their mutual well-being. They would share the same reality, which would be a self-actualizing world rather than a dehumanizing conceptual world. A collective consciousness of this order of magnitude is beyond our comprehension at this stage, but it is ours to reach for or to reject, and the time for the decision is now. We must actively assume responsibility for our own destiny.

What of the future? Studies of human behavior are now taking a new orientation. The practice and theory of Yoga and transcendental meditation, for example, have been opened to scientific analysis by the Pavlovian theory of corticovisceral (mind-body) interrelationships (Kurtsin, 1968) and also by studies of the operant conditioning of autonomic responses (Miller, 1969). Certainly this area of research, involving exploration and actualization of human potentials and awareness, takes us a long way from animal models. Perhaps the fruits of such research might give us a greater appreciation and concern not only for each other but also for animals that today are misused in many unnecessary laboratory experiments, are abused in zoos and on livestock farms, and are threatened with extinction in the wild.

I think at this stage of human endeavor and inquiry we

Conclusions

should seriously scrutinize the nature, purpose, and underlying motives involved in research with animal and human subjects in terms of ecological and social priorities. For example, studying wolf behavior and publishing one's findings in journals which few read is questionable when in ten years there may be no wolves left in the wild. Priorities and values change when a greater whole is perceived beyond one's own limited egosphere. The comparative study of animal and human behavior can broaden one's perceptual world and can increase one's personal awareness and appreciation for both "others" and "self." Since all things are related in the ecosphere (as distinct from the isolation and chaos of the highly individualized egosphere), an understanding of the parts alone is insufficient. We must begin to comprehend the relationships between gestalten (parts) and gestalts (wholes). This is true for all areas of scientific inquiry. It is also true in terms of our relationships with our fellows and with nature; alienation and ignorance underlie both genocide and ecocide. Education is needed to foster a global awareness that "all is one" and to reveal a common passion unifying humankind. The knowledge gained from scientific inquiry can help us to this end or, rather, this beginning.

ABOUT THE AUTHOR

Michael W. Fox was born in Bolton, England. After obtaining his professional degree (B.Vet.Med, M.R.C.V.S.) from the Royal Veterinary College, University of London, and his Ph.D. from the same university, he joined the faculty of Washington University in St. Louis, Missouri, in 1967 and also became the associate director of research at the St. Louis Zoo. He is recognized internationally for his work in ethology, much of which is based on studies of wolves, foxes, and domestic dogs.

He is a founding member of the British Veterinary Ethology Society and served as chairman of the National Research Council Committee on Laboratory Animal Ethology. Dr. Fox was awarded the D.Sc. degree by London University for his research in ethology in 1976, at which time he joined The Humane Society of the United States in Washington, D.C., as scientific director. Having served as vice president of bioethics, he is currently senior advisor, Office of the President, with this Society. He is also vice president for bioethics, The Humane Society International.

REFERENCES

Anonymous (1966). One or many animals in a cage? *Nutr. Rev.* 24:116–119.
Barnett, S. A., and J. Burns (1967). Early stimulation and maternal behavior. *Nature* 213:150.
Beach, F. A., and B. J. LeBoeuf (1967). Coital behavior in dogs. 1. Preferential mating in the bitch. *Anim. Behav.* 15:546–558.
Bekoff, M. (1973). The development of social interaction, play, and metacommunication in mammals; an ethological perspective. *Quart. Rev. Biol.* 47:412–434.
Bennett, E. L., M. C. Diamond, M. R. Rosenzweig, and D. Krech (1964). Chemical and anatomical plasticity of brain. *Science* 146:610–619.
Berkson, G. (1968). Development of abnormal stereotyped behaviors. *Develop. Psychobiol.* 1:118–132.
Beylaev, D. K., and L. N. Trut (1974). Some genetic and endocrine effects of selection for domestication in silver foxes. In M. W. Fox (ed.), *The wild canids*. Malabar, Fla.: Krieger.
Birdwhistell, R. L. (1970). *Kinesics and context*. Philadelphia: University of Pennsylvania Press.
Blest, A. D. (1967). The function of eyespot patterns in Lepidoptera. *Behavior* 11:209–256.
Bowlby, J. (1971). *Attachment*. London: Penguin.
Bryant, M. J. (1972). The social environment: Behavior and stress in housed livestock. *Vet. Rec.* 90:351–358.
Burghardt, G. M. In press. Amending Tinbergen: A fifth aim for ethology. In: Mitchell, R. W., Thompson, N. S., and H. L. Miles (eds.), *Anthropomorphism, Anecdotes, and Animals: The Emperor's New Clothes*. New York: SUNY Press.
Burns, M., and M. N. Fraser (1966). *Genetics of the dog*. London: Oliver and Boyd.
Candland, D. K., and D. C. Bryan, B. L. Nuzar, K. J. Kopf, and M. Sendor (1970). Squirrel monkey heart rate during formation of status orders. *J. Comp. Physiol. Psychol.* 70:417–423.
Chess, S. (1969). *Introduction to child psychiatry*. New York: Grune and Stratton.
Christian, J. J., and D. E. Davis (1964). Endocrines, behavior, and population. *Science* 146:1550–1560.

Concepts in Ethology

Conn, P. M. (ed.). 1993. *Paradigms for the Study of Behavior*. San Diego, CA: Academic Press.
Crook, J. H. (1970). *Social behavior of birds and mammals*. New York: Academic Press.
Denenberg, V. H. (1964). Critical periods, stimulation input, and emotional reactivity: A theory of infantile stimulation. *Psych. Rev.* 71:335–351.
——— (1967). Stimulation in infancy, emotional reactivity, and exploratory behavior. In D. H. Glass (ed.), *Biology and behavior: Neurosphysiology and emotion*. New York: Rockefeller University Press.
Denenberg, V. H., and A. C. Whimbey (1963). Infantile stimulation and animal husbandry: A methodological study. *J. Comp. Physiol. Psychol.* 56:877–878.
Duncan, S., Jr. (1969). Nonverbal communication. *Psych. Bull.* 72:118–137.
Eibl-Eibesfeldt, I. (1970). *Ethology—the biology of behavior*. New York: Holt, Rinehart, and Winston.
——— (1972). *Love and hate*. New York: Holt, Rinehart, and Winston. Ekman, P., and W. V. Friesen (1969). The repertoire of nonverbal behavior: Categories, origins, usage, and coding. *Semiotica* 1:49–98.
Ewbank, R. (1968). The behaviour of animals in restraint. In M. W. Fox (ed.), *Abnormal behavior in animals*. Philadelphia: W. B. Saunders.
Fox, M. W. (1967). The place and future of animal behavior studies in veterinary medicine. *J. Amer. Vet. Med. Assoc.* 151:609–615.
——— (1968). Socialization, environmental factors, and abnormal behavioral development in animals. In M. W. Fox (ed.), *Abnormal behavior in animals*. Philadelphia: W. B. Saunders.
——— (1971a). *Behavior of wolves, dogs, and related canids*. Malabar, Fla.: Krieger.
——— (1971b). *Integrative development of brain and behavior in the dog*. Chicago: University of Chicago Press.
——— (1972a). Effects of rearing conditions on behavior of laboratory animals. In *Defining the laboratory animal*, pp. 294–312. Nat. Acad. Sci., Washington D. C.
——— (1972b). *Understanding your dog*. New York: Coward McCann.
——— (1973). The place of animal behavior in the biology and psychology undergraduate curriculum. In M. W. Fox (ed.), *Readings in ethology and comparative psychology*. California: Brooks/Cole.
——— (1974). Evolution of behavior in Canidae. In M. W. Fox (ed.), *The wild canids*. Malabar, Fla.: Krieger
Fox, M. W., and R. V. Andrews (1973). Physiological and biochemical correlates of individual differences in behavior of wolf cubs. *Behaviour* 66:129–140.
Fuller, J. L. (1967). Experiential deprivation and late behaviour. *Science* 158: 1645–1652.
Gardner, R. A., and B. T. Gardner (1969). Teaching sign language to a chimpanzee. *Science* 165:664–672.
Gibbons, Jr., E. F., Wyers, E. J., Waters, E. and E. W. Menzel, Jr. (eds.). 1994. *Naturalistic Environments in Captivity for Animal Behavior Research*. Albany, NY: SUNY Press.
Ginsburg, B. E. (1968). Genotypic factors in the ontogeny of behavior. In J. H. Masserman (ed.), *Science and Psychoanalysis*, vol. 12. New York: Grune and Stratton.
Gleason, K. K., and D. Reynierse (1969). The behavioral significance of pheromones in vertebrates. *Psych. Bull.* 71:58–73.
Hall, E. T. (1969). *The hidden dimension*. New York: Doubleday.

References

Harlow, H. F. (1965). Total social isolation: Effects on macaque monkey behavior. *Science* 148:666.
Hediger, H. (1950). *Wild animals in captivity*. London: Butterworth.
Henderson, N. (1970). Genetic influences on the behavior of mice can be obscured by laboratory rearing. *J. Comp. Physiol. Psychol.* 72:505–511.
Hess, E. H. (1965). Attitude and pupil size. *Sci. Amer.* 212:46–54.
Hinde, R. A., Y. Spencer-Booth, and M. Bruce (1966). Effects of 6-day maternal deprivation on rhesus monkey infants. *Nature* 210:1021–1023.
Holzapfel, M. (1968). Abnormal behavior in zoo animals. In M. W. Fox (ed.), *Abnormal behavior in animals*. Philadelphia: W. B. Saunders.
Hutt, S. J., C. Hutt, D. Lee, and C. Ounsted (1965). A behavioral and electroencephalographic study of autistic children. *J. Psychiat. Res.* 3: 181–197.
Jensen, G. D., and R. A. Bobbitt (1968). Implications of primate research for understanding infant development. In J. H. Masserman (ed.), *Science and Psychoanalysis*, vol. 12. New York: Grune and Stratton.
Joffe, J. M. (1969). *Prenatal determinants of behavior*. New York: Pergamon Press.
Kaufman, I. C., and L. A. Rosenblum (1967). Depression in infant monkeys separated from their mothers. *Science* 155:1030.
Kavanau, J. L. (1964). Behavior: Confinement, adaptation, and compulsory regimes in laboratory rats. *Science* 143:490.
Klinghammer, E. (1967). Factors influencing choice of mate in altricial birds. In H. W. Stephenson, E. H. Hess, and H. L. Rheingold (eds.), *Early behavior*. New York: John Wiley and Sons.
Klinghammer, E., and M. W. Fox (1971). Ethology and its place in animal science. *J. Anim. Sci.* 32:1278–1283.
Krecek, J. (1971). The theory of critical developmental periods and post-natal development of endocrine functions. In E. Tobach, L. Aronson, and E. Shaw (eds.), *The biopsychology of development*. New York: Academic Press.
Kümmer, H. (1971). *Primate societies*. Chicago: Aldine.
Kurtsin, I. T. (1968). Physiological mechanisms of behavior disturbances and corticovisceral interrelations in animals. In M. W. Fox (ed.), *Abnormal behavior in animals*. Philadelphia: W. B. Saunders.
Lee, R., and I. DeVore (1968). *Man the hunter*. Chicago: Aldine.
Levine, S., and R. F. Mullins, Jr. (1966). Hormone influences on brain organization in infant rats. *Science* 152:1585–1592.
Lorenz, K. (1970). *Studies in animal and human behavior*, vol. 1. Cambridge, Mass.: Harvard University Press.
——— (1971). *Studies in animal and human behavior*, vol. 2. Cambridge, Mass.: Harvard University Press.
McCall, R. B., M. L. Lester, and C. M. Corter (1969). Caretaker effect on rats. *Develop. Psychol.* 1(6):771.
Markowitz, H. 1982. *Behavioral Enrichment in the Zoo*. New York: Van Nostrand Reinhold.
Marsden, H. M., and F. H. Bronson (1964). Strange male block to pregnancy: Its absence in inbred mouse strains. *Nature* 207:878.
Maslow, A. H. (1968). *Toward a psychology of being*. New York: Van Nostrand Reinhold.
Mason, W. A. (1967). Motivational aspects of social responsiveness in young chimpanzees. In H. W. Stevenson, E. H. Hess, and H. L. Rheingold (eds.), *Early behavior*. New York: John Wiley and Sons.

Concepts in Ethology

Mehrabian, A. (1969). Significance of posture and position in communication of attitude and status relationships. *Psych. Bull.* 71:359–372.
Meier, G. W. (1961). Infantile handling and development in Siamese kittens. *J. Comp. Physiol. Psychol.* 54:284–286.
Melzack, R., and T. H. Scott (1957). The effects of early experience on response to pain. *J. Comp. Physiol. Psychol.* 50:155–161.
Michael, R. P., and E. B. Keverne (1970). Primate sex pheromones of vaginal origin. *Nature* 225:84–85.
Miller, N. E. (1969). Learning of visceral and glandular responses. *Science* 163:434–445.
Mirsky, A. (1968). In J. H. Masserman (ed.), *Science and Psychoanalysis*, vol. 12 (discussion, pp. 112–118). New York: Grune and Stratton.
Mitchell, G. (1970). Abnormal behavior in primates. In L. A. Rosenblum (ed.), *Primate behavior*, vol. 1. New York: Academic Press.
Morris, D. (1966). Abnormal rituals in stress situations. *Phil. Trans. Roy. Soc. Lond.* (Series B) 251:327–330.
Morton, D. B., Burghardt, G. M. and J. A. Smith. 1990. Critical anthropomorphism, animal suffering, and the ecological context. *Hastings Center Report* 20(3) special supplement on Animals, Science, and Ethics:13–19.
Morton, J. R. (1968). Effects of early experience, handling, and gentling in laboratory animals. In M. W. Fox (ed.), *Abnormal behavior in animals*. Philadelphia: W. B. Saunders.
Premack, D. (1971). Language in chimpanzee? *Science* 172:808–822.
Richter, C. P. (1954). The effects of domestication and selection on the behavior of the Norway rat. *J. Nat. Cancer Inst.* 15:727–738.
Rudyar, D. (1972). *The planetarization of consciousness*. New York: Harper and Row.
Sackett, G. P. (1968). Abnormal behavior in laboratory-reared rhesus monkeys. In M. W. Fox (ed.), *Abnormal behavior in animals*. Philadelphia: W. B. Saunders.
Sackett, G. P., M. Porter, and H. Holmes (1965). Choice behavior in rhesus monkeys: Effect of stimulation during the first month of life. *Science* 147:304–306.
Salzen, E. A., and J. M. Cornell (1968). Sel-perception and species recognition in birds, Behaviour 30:44–65.
Schenkel, R. (1947). Ausdrucks-studien an Wolfen. *Behaviour* 1:81–129.
Schneirla, T. C. (1965). Aspects of stimulation and organization in approach/withdrawal processes underlying vertebrate behavioral development. In D. S. Lehrman, R. A. Hinde, and E. Shaw (eds.), *Advances in the study of animal behavior*. New York: Academic Press.
Schutz, F. (1965). Sexuelle Prägung bei Anatiden. *Z. Tierpsychol.* 22:50–103.
Scott, J. P., and J. L. Fuller (1965). *Genetics and social behavior of the dog*. Chicago: University of Chicago Press.
Sluckin, W. (1965). *Imprinting and early learning*. Chicago: Aldine.
Sommer, R. (1969). *Personal space*. Englewood Cliffs, N. J.: Prentice-Hall.
Spitz, R. (1949). The role of ecological factors in emotional development. *Child Develop.* 20:145–155.
Teilhard de Chardin, P. (1971). *Man's place in nature*. London: Fontana.
Thomas, A., S. Chess, and H. G. Birch (1970). The origin of personality. *Sci. Amer.* 223:102–109.

References

Thompson, W. R. (1957). Influence of prenatal maternal anxiety on emotionality in young rats. *Science* 125:698–699.
Thorpe, W. H. (1956). *Learning and instinct in animals.* Cambridge, England: Cambridge University Press.
Tinbergen, N. (1950). *The study of instinct.* Oxford: Clarendon Press.
Vandenbergh, J. G. (1969). Male odor accelerates female sexual maturation in mice. *Endocrinol.* 84:658–660.
Van Hooff, J. A. R. A. M. (1967). The facial displays of catarrhine monkeys and apes. In D. Morris (ed.), *Primate ethology.* Chicago: Aldine.
White, J. (1972). *The highest state of consciousness.* New York: Doubleday.
Wickler, W. (1972). *The sexual code.* New York: Doubleday.
Woolpy, J. H. (1968). Socialization of wolves. In J. H. Masserman (ed.), *Science and Psychoanalysis*, vol. 12. New York: Grune and Stratton.
Zimen, E. (1974) Social dynamics of captive wolf packs. In M. W. Fox (ed.), *The wild canids.* Malabar, Fla.: Krieger.

BIBLIOGRAPHY

Alcock, J. (1984). *Animal Behavior: An evolutionary approach.* Sunderland, MA: Sinauer Associates Inc.
Allen, C., and M. Bekoff (1997). *Species of mind: The philosophy and biology of cognitive ethology.* Cambridge, MA: MIT Press.
Barber, T. X. (1993). *The human nature of birds: A scientific discovery with startling implications.* New York: St. Martin's Press.
Beaver, B. V. (1994). *The veterinarian encyclopedia of animal behavior.* Ames, IA: State University Press.
Beck, A., and A. Katcher (1996). *Between pets and people: The importance of animal companionship.* Revised edition. West Lafayette, IN: Purdue University Press. (contains list of worldwide sites as of 1996).
Bekoff, M., and D. Jamieson (eds.) (1996). *Readings in animal cognition.* Cambridge, MA: MIT Press.
Bonner, J. T. (1980). *The evolution of culture in animals.* Princeton, NJ: Princeton University Press.
Broom, D. M., and K. G. Johnson (1993). *Stress and animal welfare.* New York: Chapman & Hall.
Candland, D. K. (1965). *Feral children & clever animals: Reflections on human nature.* Oxford, England: Oxford University Press.
Craig, J. V. (1981). *Domestic animal behavior.* Englewood Cliffs, NJ: Prentice Hall.
Dawkins, M. S. (1980). *Animal suffering: The science of animal welfare.* New York: Routledge, Chapman and Hall.
Dawkins, M. S. (1993). *Through our eyes only?* San Francisco: W. H. Freeman.
DeGrazia, D. (1996). *Taking animals seriously: Mental life and moral status.* Cambridge, MA: Cambridge University Press.
Dol, M., S. Kasamoentalib, S. Lijmbach, E. Rivas, and R. van den Bos (eds.) (1997). *Animal consciousness and animal ethics,* VanGorcum, Assen.
Estes, R. D. (1992). *The behavior guide to African mammals.* Berkeley, CA: University of California Press.
Fraser, A. F., and D. M. Broom (1990). *Farm animal behavior and welfare.* Philadelphia, PA: Bailliere Tindall.

Concepts in Ethology

Gittleman, J. L., (ed.) (1996). *Carnivore behavior, ecology, and evolution.* Ithaca, NY: Cornell University Press.
Gould, J. L., and C. G. Gould (1994). *The animal mind.* New York: Scientific American Library.
Griffin, D. (1992). *Animal minds.* Chicago, IL: University of Chicago Press.
Harre, R., and V. Reynolds (eds.) (1984). *The meaning of primate signals.* Cambridge, England: Cambridge University Press.
Hart, L. (ed.) (1997). *Responsible conduct of research in animal behavior.* New York: Oxford University Press.
Hoage, R. J., and L. Goldman (eds.), (1986). *Animal intelligence: insights into the animal mind.* Washington, DC: Smithsonian Institution Press.
Honore, E. K., and P. H. Klopfer (1990). *A Concise survey of animal behavior.* San Diego, CA: Academic Press/Harcourt Brace Janovich.
Houpt, K. A. (1991). *Domestic animal behavior.* Ames, IA: State University Press.
Kilgour, R., and C. Dalton (1984). *Livestock behavior: A practical guide.* New York: Granada.
Lawrence, A. B., and J. Rushen (eds.) (1993). *Stereotypic animal behaviour: Fundamentals and applications to welfare.* Wallingford, Oxon, England: CAB International.
Linden, E. (1986). *Silent partner: The legacy of the ape language experiments.* New York: Time Books.
McFarland, D. (ed.) (1982). *The oxford companion to animal behavior.* New York: Oxford University Press.
Manning, A., and J. Serpell (eds.) (1994). *Animals and human society: Changing perspectives.* New York: Routledge.
Masson, J. M., and S. McCarthy (1995). *When elephants weep: The emotional lives of animals.* New York: Delacourte Press.
Mitchell, R. W., and N. S. Thompson (1986). *Deception: Perspectives on human and nonhuman deceit.* Albany, NY: State University of New York Press.
Nollman, J. (1987). *Animal dreaming: The art and science of interspecies communication.* Toronto and New York: Bantam Books.
North East Regional Agricultural Engineering Service (1995). *Animal behavior and the design of livestock and poultry systems.* Conference Proceedings NRAES-84. Ithaca, NY: NERAES Cooperative Extension, 152 Riley, Robb Hall.
Phillips, C., and D. Piggins (ed) (1992). *Farm animals and the environment.* Wallingford Oxford: C.A.B. International.
Ristau, C. A. (ed.) (1991). *Cognitive ethology: The minds of other animals (Essays in Honor of Donald R. Griffin).* NJ: Lawrence Erlbaum Associates.
Rollin, B. E. (1989). *The unheeded cry: Animal consciousness, animal pain and science.* New York: Oxford University Press.
Rollin, B. E. (1995). *Farm animal welfare: Social, bioethical, and research issues.* Ames, IA: Iowa State University Press.
Serpell, J. (1996). *In the company of animals: A study of human-animal relationships.* New York: Cambridge University Press.
Skutch, A. F. (1996). *The minds of birds.* College Station, TX: Texas A&M University Press.
de Waal, F. (1996). *Good natured: The origins of right and wrong in humans and other animals.* Cambridge, MA: Harvard University Press.
Webster, J. (1994). *Animal welfare: A cool eye toward eden.* New York: Blackwell.
Wood-Gush, D. G. M. (1983). *Elements of ethology.* New York: Chapman & Hall.

INDEX

aggression: 35–36; ritualized, 40–41; and territory, 52
ahimsa, 119
altruism, 18, 27–28, 40
Andrews, R. V., 37
animal feelings, 113–131
animal healing, 116–117
animal husbandry, 83–90
animal protection laws, 135
animal rights, 124, 138
animal suffering, 117–118
approach-withdrawal processes, 62–64
autism, 75, 76, 77
autonomic "tuning," 64–68

Barnett, S. A., 109
Beach, F. A., 50
Bekoff, M., 19
Bennett, E. L., 71, 95
Berkson, G., 73
Berry, T., 126, 129
Beylaev, D. K., 51
bioethics, 121, 132–140
biomedical research, 138
Birch, H. G., 37, 68
Birdwhistell, R. L., 20
Blest, A. D., 9
Bobbitt, R. A., 74
body language, 19–22
bond, human-animal, 113–131, 137
Bowlby, J., 61–62, 79
Bronson, F. H., 22, 94

Bruce effect, 22, 94
Bryant, M. J., 83
Burns, M., 101, 109

Candland, D. K., 37
chemical communication, 22–24
Chess, S., 37, 68, 80
children: socialization of, 61–62
Christian, J. J., 94
circadian variables, 102–104
communication: in wolves, 43–45
compassion, 139
compromise postures, 14–16
consciousness, evolution, 145
Cornell, J. M., 58
Corter, C. M., 101
courtship displacements, 12–13
critical distance, 25–26
critical period, 56, 60, 61
Crook, J. H., 31
crowding stress, 24, 54, 89, 93–94

Davis, D. E., 93
Denenberg, V. H., 65, 66, 97
derived activities: 16–19; in wolves, 40, 41, 42
DeVore, I., 47
displacement behaviors, 12–14
distraction displays, 14–15
dogs: comparisons with wolves, 49–53
domestication: effects of, 49–54, 84–85

161

dominance: and heart rate, 36–37; and early experience, 68
Duncan, S., Jr., 20

early rearing: and sociability, 58–59; and development, 62–80
ecos, 121–122, 137
EEG: effect of handling on, 67, 68; effect of isolation on, 76
Eibl-Eibesfeldt, I., 19, 20
Ekman, P., 13, 22
empathy, 114, 116, 125–126, 132
ethology: history of, 3–5; applied, 5
ethos, 121–122, 137
Ewbank, R., 87
experimental variables, 92–104, 108–112

facial expressions: in canids, 44–46
farm animals, 83–90, 137
feral vision, 126–128
flight distance, 25–26
Fox, M. W., 5, 30, 33, 34, 35, 37, 39, 42, 43, 45, 50, 52, 56, 58, 67, 72, 76, 77, 78, 79, 80, 84, 86, 90, 91, 95, 110, 111
Fraser, A., xxi, 138
Fraser, M. N., 101
Friesen, W. V., 13, 22
Fuller, J. L., 53, 60, 75

Gardner, B. T., 29
Gardner, R. A., 29
genetics: and specialization, 53; and handling stress, 66–67, 69; interaction of, with environment, 78
Ginsburg, B. E., 66
Gleason, K. K., 22
Griffin, D., xx

Hall, E. T., 21, 22, 23
handling effects, 65–71
Harlow, H. F., 63, 74, 79
Hediger, H., 25, 56, 91
Henderson, N., 78
Hess, E. H., 11–12
Hinde, R. A., 79
Holmes, H., 59
Holzapfel, M., 73, 91
human development, 143–144

human ethology, 19–22
Hutt, S. J., 77

imprinting, 56–62, 86
individualism, 146
institutionalization syndrome, 72
intelligence: and trainability, 53; and exploration, 77
isolation: effects of, on development, 73–77

Jensen, G. D., 74
Joffe, J. M., 69

Kavanau, J. L., 95
Keverne, E. B., 24
Klinghammer, E., 5, 57, 83, 85
Krecek, J., 109
Kümmer, H., 32
Kurtsin, I. T., 111, 148

laboratory animals, 67, 78, 92–112
LeBoeuf, B. J., 50
Lee, R., 47
Lee-Boot effect, 23
Lester, M. L., 101
Levine, S., 66
Lorenz, K., xxii, 12, 56

McCall, R. B., 101
Marsden, H. M., 22, 94
Maslow, A. H., 144
Mason, W. A., 73
Mehrabian, A., 20
Meier, G., 68
Melzack, R., 76
metacommunication, 19–22
Michael, R. P., 24
Miller, N. E., 148
Mirsky, A., 73
Mitchell, G., 79
morality, 132
Morris, D., 91
Morton, J. R., 94
Mullins, R. F., 66

pheromones, 22–24
Porter, M., 59
Potter, V. R., 133
Premack, D., 29
prenatal influences, 68–71

Index

releasers, 6–12
Reynierse, D., 22
Richter, C. P., 51, 93
Rosenblum, L. A., 78, 79
Rudyar, D., 147

Sackett, G. P., 59, 73, 74
Salzen, E. A., 58
Schenkel, R., 29
Schneirla, T. C., 62
Schutz, F., 57
Schwabe, C., 119
Schweitzer, A., 138
Scott, J. P., 53, 60
Scott, T. H., 76
sex: and domestication, 49–50; and aggression, 52–53; and imprinting, 56–57
sign stimuli, 6–12
Sluckin, W., 85
social deprivation: and development, 73–78
socialization: 56, 62; and trainability 53; and restraint, 105
social spacing, 21–22
sociosexual activities, 16–19
Sommer, R., 22, 26
Spitz, R., 11, 63, 79
stereotyped activities, 72, 75
symbiotic harmony, 137

Teilhard de Chardin, P., 27, 129, 147

telos, xx, 121–122, 137
temperament: in canids, 33–37
territoriality, 24–25
Thomas, A., 37, 68
Thompson, W. R., 69
Thorpe, W. H., 11
Tiger, L., 48
Tinbergen, N., 6, 8, 14
tool-using, 28, 29
Trut, L. N., 51

vaginal pheromones, 24
Vandenbergh, J. G., 108
Van Hooff, J. A. R. A. M., 44
vivisection, 138

Waal, F. de, 132
Whimbey, A. C., 97
White, J., 29
Whitten effect, 23
Wickler, W., 18
Wilson, E. O., xx
wolves: rituals of, 38–39; social relationships in, 38; communication in, 43–45
Woolpy, J. H., 61
World Trade Organization, 147

Zimen, E., 38
zoo animals: propagation of, 91–92, 96